THIS IS ME

BEATING THE ODDS

FINN FOSTER

Edited by Brooks Becker

Cover design: Finn Foster

Cover photo: Live Elevated Inc.

First paperback edition August 2021

ISBN: 978-0-578-91643-9

Published by Live Elevated Inc.
www.finnfoster.com

THIS BOOK IS DEDICATED TO MY MOM AND DAD,

I LOVE YOU.

CONTENTS

Prologue

Hey there! My name is Finn, and I'm so glad you chose to read my book. I am beyond excited to see how this book will connect with you. When I initially started writing, I wasn't sure how I was going to deliver my message. I would find myself writing down my ideas and thought bubbles, but I would become easily discouraged when I couldn't get more than a few words jotted down. After a year, I finally started brainstorming and focusing on a center point based on a question I kept asking myself: How can I reach as many people as possible with my story? Social Media was an option, but not my go to. So I continued to pioneer other ideas. One day it came to me: a book. Whether or not you believe it, every single one of you is amazing! I encourage you to find some time to acknowledge that. I understand hearing it and knowing it aren't the same thing, but I urge you to embrace yourself. It took me some time to acknowledge that inner voice to remind me that I am amazing. However, finding this clarity is such a refreshing experience. I hope by the end of this book, you'll remember what I just told you. You are truly amazing.

Years ago, I was periodically dragged down by negative events and experiences in my life. Because of this, I sought to find the solutions to these struggles. I realized that doing your best, and seeking the opportunity to change and grow, would be optimal for my development and character. At the time, my life was consumed by anger and negativity. I lost sight of my focus, goals, and dreams and then drifted further and further away from reaching them. I was once told that throughout life, we will face obstacles that will challenge us, make us or break us, but most importantly develop us to reach our greatest potential.

Some of you are reading this book because you were interested in the title. Some of you are experiencing a hardship or even a handful of hardships. Some of you know me personally and wanted to support my purpose, and I appreciate it. Some of you are looking for answers. Some of you are looking for hope. Some of you just want a motivational read, and that is admirable. There are endless ways you may have come across this book and started reading. I hope through reading this book you come to understand what victory feels and sounds like; not my victory, but YOUR victory. We each have a story and it just so happened you stumbled across mine. I am praying that through this book you will connect with me and understand that we all are much more related to one another than you may have thought. Each of us gets the same twenty-four hours in a day, and we get a choice to do big things or little things with that time. Perhaps this is the season in which you want to do big things in your life, become more mindful about your choices, dreams and goals. Perhaps your struggles are holding you back, and you seek to overcome and break through. Well, this is your season. Embrace it!

In the years leading up to the publication of my book, I struggled to share parts of my story. Mostly because I was afraid people wouldn't understand me or perhaps they would think I was crazy. I prayed and thought it through before I became at ease with myself sharing parts of my life that are more in depth emotionally. I realized too many people only share 90 percent of themselves, and it's the 10 percent we leave out that holds the greatest impact. There will be times that people may not understand what you are going through, and that's OK. Life is a marathon, not a race. Yes, we are all running to the finish line, but not everyone is running at the same pace. That's the beauty about this journey called life. We can run it as fast or as slow as we choose. Take your time, but don't waste your time. At the end of the day, your pace should not be defined by those around you.

I want to challenge you to focus and develop a mindset to execute on all the dreams, goals, and opportunities that you have pondered, planned, and held back from achieving. Too many times I found myself thinking, questioning, and debating whether or not I can accomplish my goals. Once I figured out that the only person holding me back was myself, I wanted to change. No one person on this earth can be better at being themselves by doing nothing. I guarantee if you sat down and spent some time with your friends soaking up their life experiences, you'd find that they each have something they can relate to with you. I have spoken with a lot people over the past few years and sometimes I think we become afraid or too self-conscious about what others possibly think of us. Perhaps the uncertainty of a specific situation could make us feel a bit uncomfortable or embarrassed. This is of course a normal response. Later on you'll come across a chapter that goes into depth about vulnerability and how it lead me to connect with people.

There have been times that I've had to sit down and truly analyze myself. I have looked at my life in episodes. I have come to appreciate the struggles and the leaps of life. Someone once told me that life will come at you hard and you have to be willing to face it. I believe I mentioned one of the greatest setbacks for publishing my book was not digging deep enough into my story and really elaborating about it. I once read a quote by Theodore Roosevelt that really gets my feelings across: "It is not the critic who counts; not the man who points out how the strong man stumbles, or where the doer of deeds could have done them better. The credit belongs to the man who is actually in the arena, whose face is marred by dust and sweat and blood; who strives valiantly; who errs, who comes short again and again, because there is no effort without error and shortcoming; but who does actually strive to do the deeds; who knows great enthusiasms, the great devotions; who spends himself in a worthy cause; who at the best knows in the end the triumph of high achievement, and who at the worst, if he fails, at least fails while daring greatly, so that his place shall never be with those cold and timid souls who neither know victory nor defeat."

I don't have it all figured out, but what we have to know is that everything you and I go through is intentional and can be figured out if we choose to. The moment you learn to break down and let go and approach everything in life with a victorious approach, you may see people around you start re-engage their focus to change as well. Your breakthrough may just be the reason why they wanted to overcome. All too often, we don't dig deep enough into parts of our lives because of fear. It holds us back more often than not because we are thinking about what others may think of us. You feel that it may shake your worth as a person. Honestly though, people need to hear the raw. I don't care what walk in life you are on at this very moment, you and I are both broken. That means no man or woman is better or worse than the next. Open your eyes and ears to embrace and acknowledge the moments you have been locking up. Understand that those are the pieces that will bring healing and hope. I always tell people that we are a giant puzzle. Each piece is one of us. every single piece is needed in order to complete the puzzle. You are important, and even those raw and deep emotions we have, the moments that we do our best to forget and pack away so we never see them again, those are the moments that people will say, "Man, I've been there. I want to overcome. I want to be joyful." Your healing becomes contagious and others will seek it as well.

One of the greatest soccer players in the world, Lionel Messi, is a legend who plays ball like no other. However, he didn't become successful overnight. It took him 17 years and 114 days to become an on overnight success. Day in, and day out he would practice the drills over and over again. No matter how tired he was, no matter how good he was getting, he wanted to create consistency. While he became the world's greatest, he was judged, rejected, and often ridiculed when he first started playing in the pros. But Messi never allowed those words or people to slow him down. A friend once told me to hustle until your haters ask if you are hiring. It's so true—people will do the best to bring you down because they may not understand the shift you are taking. Messi is now known to be a legend and all-time best. Life is all about the challenges we face, it's how you adapt to them and use them to grow. Some of you will be in a season in which you feel like you are not moving. You may be in a season where you might not understand why you are in the very place that you are in. Throughout this book, throughout this season of reading, you will begin to understand why I live life the way I do. At one point in my own life, I didn't see the silver lining, I didn't know where I would end up, I didn't have motivation to change and grow. But at some point you just have to take the leap and hope you land on your feet. You miss 100 percent of the shots you never take. Life is all about opportunities, and if this book is your opportunity, then go for it!

So, why did I write this book? To tell you that standing in the arena and getting my butt whooped on occasion is part of the journey. You got to get up and go at it until you've won! One of the greatest feelings in life is when you can say, "I am victorious about my life. I'm victorious about the strides that I'm taking." I am beyond excited for you as you learn more about who you are. I wasn't always a driven individual, however over the past years I become aware of my journey, my experiences and wanted to help people navigate through their struggles and overcome as well. Not everyone has the same story, but we all have one. By doing so, I figured this book would be one of many ways I could reach people. With intentions to inspire and encourage people, I wrote this book with different elements of writing to deliver a transparent perspective. I hope this book will remind you how amazing you are. It took me several years to produce this book, but it was worth the time, endless amount of nights where I stayed up to dig into my story for you. Be blessed, continue smile, and remember you are amazing!

Chapter 1 | Laying the Foundation

It is another beautiful fall day, finally the air is cool and crisp again and most everywhere I go I see people wearing their sweaters and sipping on a fall favorite: Pumpkin Spice Latte. Where do I begin, though? Great question. Well, If you know me, I am always stirring up a conversation with someone wherever I go. I just happened to be at the local coffee shop one morning to grab a cup of coffee and said good morning to the barista behind the counter. Of course knowing me, I always like to see how people are doing, so I asked her how she was and thankfully not too many people were there that morning. We were able to talk for a while. I'm known to say corny dad jokes, and of course I couldn't hold back. We both started laughing and she glanced at me and said, "You are funny, wish more people like you would come through here." I blushed and of course was startled by the comment. Well, I told her if she was free to sit down at my table, then she was welcome to join me. She was able to get a quick 15 minute break and joined me while exchanging names and sharing a bit about each other. She had shared where she grew up, and what she wanted to do when she got done with school. Something about her just made me feel so warm inside. We went on about our conversation and she realized that her 15 minute break was up. She smiled at me and made her way back to her work area. I smiled back and waved timidly. I sat there and pondered what had just happened. I took my last sip of coffee and made my way up to say goodbye to the barista and I would see her again soon.

Months went by, and I had been to that little coffee shop about three dozen more times since my first time going. Just like most days I walked in, said hello, and got my usual cup of Joe. I then of course would proceed to my favorite table in the coffee shop. It had been a bit busier that day, and I knew the barista was preoccupied serving people coffee, and so I didn't want to hold her up from working. She smiled at me and said, "I hope you have a nice day!" I responded with the same and told her how awesome she was. As I made my way to usual spot, I came across an older man sitting where I usually sat.

He was sipping on his cup of coffee and reading the local newspaper. I approached him and politely asked if I was able to sit with him. I liked that spot because of the views, and of course it just so happened to be the coziest spot in the tiny shop.

The old man was wearing a cap on his head that looked like it had seen better days. I asked him how his day was. He looked up at me and said, " Son, I'm doing well. This coffee is good, therefore I am a happy man." I smiled and, chuckling, I said that I agreed with him. I noticed that the man had been reading the same page of the newspaper since I had started sitting there with him. So I decided to introduce myself and ask him if he would like another cup of coffee. He smiled from ear to ear and said yes, please. I made way up to the counter to get two additional cups of coffee for the old man and myself. Moments later, I returned where the old man was seated and joined him in silence. He then put down his newspaper, took a sip of his coffee and asked me why I got him another cup of coffee. I explained to him that I saw he had finished his first cup and wanted to get him another one since I was getting one too. The man smiled and chuckled and picked up his newspaper and started reading again. I was trying to figure out what just happened. I finished my coffee and said goodbye to the older man. He said goodbye and said, "Don't stop doing what you are doing, son, you will do great things." I looked back and said thank you to him. I dropped my coffee cup in the dirty bin near the front and left for the day.

A few months had passed and it was the first week of December. I got into my car, turned on the heat, and went to get some morning joe. However, as I pulled up to the shop, I noticed a sign on the door. It said "FOR SALE" in large red letters. I got out of my car, and walked up to the coffee shop and read the sign again. I asked myself how this could be? I hadn't been to the shop in a few weeks and it was certainly a very popular place for many of the locals. I stood there for a second and reminisced, simply soaking up the fact that a gathering place had become vacant. A familiar face was walking towards me and stood beside me with his hands in his pockets. It was a bit cooler that day but both of us were just standing there. The old man with the rugged hat chuckled and shook his head. He looked over to me and said, "Son, opportunities will arise, and people will go for them." He continued by saying, "I remember when I had to make that leap. You'll find yourself jumping and leaping for the rest of your life. That's the only way you'll ever succeed."

My friends, I would like to share with you that in your life, in your seasons of growth and elevation, sometimes you won't know where you will land when you jump. We are on the edge, we look over and hesitate because we don't know what's next. You will come across people who will speak life and motivation, and there are those who become threatened by your success, by your progress, by your character, and become uncomfortable because they are aware of the place they currently reside. I added the story about the barista, the coffee shop and the old man as a symbol, an encounter that speaks truth and life on so many levels. Throughout this book, I will share moments like that one to give you a glimpse of a real-time event that took place. Each moment we have in our life is another point of your journey. Not every moment you've been through is a positive one. Sometimes it's those tucked-away, never-touch-again moments that speak life more than you imagined. I found that with the words and experiences each of us have, we can touch and move people in greater ways than we could have imagined. For a long time I was afraid to share my story, to dig deep into some horrific moments because of how people may see me. Well, I'm going to give you this in the raw. The events in my life gave me a chance to understand that we each have a purpose, we each will promote when it's time, and that God will allow people to be in your life to elevate you. If you aren't in the arena and getting your butt whopped, then you are doing something wrong. We have to face life, our challenges, our hurts, and our vulnerabilities with courage and stand steadfast in the moments you have overcome. People will criticize and look at you funny, but don't be discouraged or scared to share those pieces that you may fear to tell. Most authors do their best to add a short story at the beginning or even the end of their book to highlight the initial spark that got them to start writing. The shifts or sparks in my life created the content to share in this book. Just because something you experience isn't a walk in the park, doesn't mean that it's of less value. It's part of you, and I urge you to use those moments to impact people. If you struggle or fear to share those parts of your life, well, I hope by the end of this book you'll have that courage to push yourself to make a difference in millions of people's lives.

I have found a deep interest in people's journeys. Since I began to understand my walk and my journey, I have greatly desired to see each person I encounter strive to develop lifelong habits to be the best version of themselves, to seek diligently by praying, and to love people in all places at all times. It wasn't long ago that I realized I wanted to be a global influencer and motivator on multiple platforms. It wasn't until just a few short years ago that I gave my life to Christ and my life took a complete 180.

Later on in the book I will share my story in two parts that will highlight that encounter I had with God. When I first started writing this book, I struggled to dig deep and reach the depth of vulnerability. It was like revisiting old memories that brought that funny feeling to your gut.

So, where do I actually begin? How should a book like this even begin? Well, I guess I should take you back as far as possible. I will take you back to when I was born based on the information that I got from my parents over the years. I was born in a very small Russian town about 2.5 hours east of Moscow by the name of Perm, on June 5, 1998. To my best knowledge I was C-sectioned from mother and immediately from birth separated from my biological mother. At some point I was placed in an orphanage where I would be for nine months. It is very common in Russia for newborn babies to be separated from their mothers at an early stage of life because she cannot care for the child properly. This can be resulted from drugs, alcohol, poverty, not able, age, legal issues...the list goes on. To this day my family and I have no extended knowledge as to why my biological mother gave me up for adoption. During the nineties, Russia was struggling economically and many people were poor, and not able to take care of themselves properly. Russia at the time was also still a very heavily communist nation, meaning families had to make do with what they had most of the time. Now it is important to note that infants are incredibly smart, and though they may not be able to talk, or make a rational decision on their own, the brain is rapidly developing from the time they are born. Furthermore, an infant is developing attachment with the mother in the first stage of life, usually the first six to nine months. Most orphanages in Russia were at times limited with staff and it was very difficult to properly care for the babies, so the amount of nourishment and attachment was very limited. Many of you know that babies cry when they need to be changed, or are hungry. This is a baby's way of communication for the first months of life. When a baby cries, the mother or father will respond to tend to the care the baby needs. For example, a baby that is hungry begins to cry. The mother hears the baby crying, she responds, and baby feels safe. Whether the mother changed or fed the baby, the baby felt safe. A significant percent of the babies in orphanages will not have an immediate response when the crying begins. While another percent will continue to cry and within forty-five minutes a response for care is executed; however, the baby doesn't feel safe. Most commonly, the baby will cry and a prolonged delayed response for care is executed. The baby will typically fall asleep due to all the energy used to cry. This becomes a horrific cycle and is very common in orphanages across the world. A baby will wake from their sleep, begin to cry, continue to cry with no response, and yet again fall back asleep.

When I got older my parents began to explain what had happened and why it happened. I guess I should better explain what was going on in my first nine months of my life. I was amongst a group of about forty or fifty other babies in the orphanage, and one caregiver would be on rotation taking care of each of us. Again, I was a baby so I don't recall the orphanage at all; however, based on my what my parents witnessed later on when they adopted me, I would cry and cry, and the caregiver would be taking care of the other babies which with no harm intended, delayed the care of the other babies including me. As Ive gotten older I was able to extend my knowledge, and comprehend the situation much better. I would then fall asleep. I would be hungry, or even my diaper was full and needed to be changed. Just like any child, or even grown up, we want attention, to be cared for and loved. Imagine a total of nine months of minimum care, minimum attention, delayed feeding and changing times for nine months. I was going through that for nine months. To be quite frank with you, I had developed a detachment issue. As I got older I became more knowledgeable of how it all took place, how the detachment developed and how it affected me is something I will elaborate on more later in the chapter.

In March of 1999, my mom and dad had spent their first week in Russia venturing around, sightseeing in the capital and celebrating my mom's birthday. The process for adoption is a very time-consuming and complicated process and must be done correctly in order for everything to fall into place. From conversations with my parents, they were anxious, and extremely excited to adopt me. For them this too was a life-changing event. To this day we celebrate March 23 as the Adoption Day, where we became family. While all of this was going on and the days were nearing to finalize everything, my dad still had six months left of his assignment in Tampa, Florida, where he served and invested in the growth and progress of the US Army.

My dad was born in small town in Ohio, the third of four kids, in April 1967. Dad grew up on a farm until he was about five years old. His parents worked in the real estate business developing residential and commercial developments. They found that Florida was a much better place to begin doing business, so a page turn in my dad's life happened. After moving down to Brandon, Florida, Dad's parents got settled and started working on growing their company that was and still is a successful one. Dad attended school locally in Brandon. He eventually made his way to a recruiter's office so he could enlist in to the US Army. Dad had gone through some rough patches during his early twenties but found clarity at twenty-five while he was on his way to Officer Candidate School (OCS). Dad worked hard on his education while he was enlisted and promoted multiple times before his commanding officer told him he was going to be an officer.

Mom was born in Germany in March of 1968. She is the youngest of two and has an older sister. Mom grew up in a small home with her parents and sister. Her parents were extremely strict and always made sure she was doing well in school, and that when she was old enough she would need to work a job. Mom had moved in with her grandparents at some point of her earlier teenage years. When Mom was eighteen years old, she had applied for a job at the Rathaus, which is the city town hall, and she was simultaneously working on her education at the university.

Over the years Mom and Dad both took their own paths in two different parts of the world focusing on their careers, and soon would find each other, falling in love. One of my favorite stories Mom and Dad always shared was when they met at the local swimming pool. Mom always had a passion for gymnastics and swimming. So one day she and some of her friends had been at the pool and she caught a glimpse of Dad. At the time, Mom spoke no English, and one of her friends had to translate for her to communicate with Dad. After six months of dating, Dad proposed and ended up marrying Mom in Oklahoma in April 1993.

Coming back to March 1999, the week of March 23, Mom and Dad began the legal process in court to adopt me. During the process, there were reports that bombing was taking place in a nearby city. The court process continued as normal and was completed in due time. Hours later, at the airport, US military personal escorted my parents and me to an airplane to board safely. To this day I look back and think, *Just what an incredible story. We have been on a journey as a family.*

The journey continued as we only had six months remaining in Florida before we would make our way to

Germany. June 5, 1999 marked a significant day in my life. Besides turning one year old, on that day I was sworn in as a US citizen. Interesting fact about that ceremony was that it took place on a Saturday, which no citizenship ceremonies take place. However, our family was celebrating my citizenship of the US. Months later we finally moved to Germany, where Dad now got his new assignment. Again, I don't recall to much of the move, and most of the events before 2000. However, while still living in Germany and finally settled, we traveled around the Mediterranean/Middle East for a two-week vacation. I believe we took a cruise and stopped in Egypt, Cypress, Israel, and Turkey. Most of the memories that I have from that vacation are found in huge photo albums put together earlier on. However, I do remember Dad reading my favorite book at the time, *Green Eggs and Ham*, while we were in Turkey.

If I remember correctly we were living in Heidelberg and I started kindergarten when I was four years old. I was growing, speaking English and German, fitting into a new shoe size every five months or so. Between Dad speaking English and Mom speaking German, I had become fluent in both. I remember living in Heidelberg very well.

I saw my Oma and Opa almost every week, and some days Dad would take me to work with him. I had all the attention in the world. I was a happy kid. Always outgoing, loved to play, laugh, and eat food! It was summer of 2002, and I remember a heat wave hit Europe hard. My mom was pregnant with my brother, who was born in October 2002. As Mom was nearing her full term, she wasn't feeling all too well and Dad was home more often to take care of her until she needed to go to the hospital for delivery. When the time came for Mom to be hospitalized, I had lived with my Oma and Opa for a bit. I of course was always worried if everything was OK with Mom. Dad would always remind me that Mom was going to be OK, and that she loved me. On October 1, my brother was born. Well, just like with any successful pregnancy, Mom and the baby stayed in the hospital for a few extra days and then went home to rest. Things went back to normal, at home, and I was going to be a big brother. Now before I continue I would like to emphasize that the events that I share with you are real. And the responses, behaviors, and emotions were all present at that time. Some of you may not quite understand all of it, but that's OK. Like I said when I started off this book, I wanted to share with you real life events that help paint a picture for you of my life.

I believe it is important to highlight that a child who experiences any form of detachment, can experience a developmental barrier of trust, and the bond between the infant and the mother. If I were to get technical, attachment is defined as the affectionate tie between two people. It all begins with the bond between an infant and the mother. And see, this bond becomes eternally representative of how the child will form the relationship with the world and the people that they expect to encounter. Now at the time when my brother was born Mom and Dad didn't even think twice that had some kind of attachment issue. Most of the behaviors and social cues were much more obvious at the age of five when I developed social skills, self-awareness and an awareness of my thoughts and feelings. However, in my case I was significantly independent but co-dependent for attention. It is important to highlight that the attachment deficiency is common amongst adopted children, however research has been much more prevalent in recent years. I know this all may not make sense, and how such behaviors can be discovered. It is vital though to know that we each struggle with attachment to some degree. I don't believe any infant, child, or adult seeks to experience poor love or poor care. One of the hardest things to talk about is my detachment I had growing up. I used to think that I was stuck, and would never overcome it. Unfortunately, there are people that have struggled to overcome their attachment deficits, and has caused them their life, relationships, and overall character. But I'm hoping that as you read on, you know that each step of the way was a key role to the person I am today. Most importantly, the parts of the story we least talk about are the parts we neglect and fail to realize gives us the drive to live and become who we are called to be. I am not a health care provider by coincidence. It is by purpose that I am living my life to help people and becoming the best version of themselves. It's not about erasing the less exciting or more negative parts of your story, it's about embracing them, and growing from those moments. It is in those moments that you will design a blueprint for others who may share the similar encounter and need to hear someone else has gone through it. Not for a second do I want people to think I stopped struggling because I overcame a significant time of my life, because that's not true. I am still learning about the wonders of my journey. Daily I take detours and seek counsel from friends and family. We become so used to tucking away our insecurities and struggles that we temporarily forget, but never truly forgive the people, the situation or even ourselves. Don't be afraid to embrace those moments that seem more ugly. Those are the common ground of mankind.

Later in this book I will elaborate more on how I went from not trusting, not loving, being angry, being afraid, and choosing to live isolated to living a life full of joy, love, zeal, purpose, passion, and faith. One must explain for others to understand; therefore, as I have mentioned before, this book contains in-depth personal encounters that I had overcome so I can coach and ultimately walk in my purpose.

By the time I was in elementary school, I had become more and more angry with my parents because I believed that they were against me. I would disobey, dishonor, and simply disrespect what they may have told me. I was deliberate about my choices and behavior. I had no remorse about the outcome or the actual situation at the time. While I was being defiant and intentional with my actions, both my parents continued to love and care for me unconditionally.

This chapter is a hard chapter for me personally because it required me to dig deep into the past where some of these events where more vivid. Furthermore, in 2003, we moved to Mons, Belgium, where Dad had been working with joint forces of NATO at SHAPE where he had been promoted from Captain (O-3) to Major (O-4) and served as an Executive Officer (XO) on behalf of his General.

At this point in my life, I was much more aware of my choices and behaviors, which honestly didn't faze me. I didn't care if Mom or Dad grounded me or gave me some type of punishment. Looking back though, it worked! I just wasn't ready at the time. I truly was afraid to be loved, or to love at this point of my life. Now, I must say there were more good days than bad. As I have mentioned before, a large percentage of adopted children are affected with some level of trust issues, fear to be loved, or to love, and lack feelings that are appropriate to certain events that may be present. I was the class clown in first grade. I would say that I enjoyed school, and playing tag during recess.

But I wasn't all too fond of my teachers. I didn't like listening to them. Children who are adopted typically struggle with authority and prefer to only listen to their own judgment. The root cause for this kind of behavior comes from the lack of attention during the developmental stages of an infant. (First 9 months of life) Again, at this time in my life I was afraid and angry. Nobody was sure why. In 2005, we had made one more move to Munster, Germany. Dad was slowly getting closer to retirement at the time, which allowed for him to be at home more often. As I have said, more good days than bad, but I was getting older and Dad just didn't think that this behavior was OK. Both Mom and Dad wanted the best for me, and they didn't give up on me. They began to read articles, books, and even spoke to professionals on the behavior of adopted children. My Mom shared with me in more recent years there were a collection of books she read by Nancy Thomas who specializes in boding and conscience development. My mom had expressed that Nancy's books had been exactly what she needed. Everything they had read and heard lined up with me and my behavior. My parents didn't realize that over the past nine to ten years I had been struggling with a detachment due to the immediate placement in an orphanage in Russia, as well as the limited to nonexistent care during my first nine months of life. It all made sense.

By 2010, Our family made some adjustments to assure that my growth and development would not be compromised going into my teens. With an increased level of discipline and structure at home, I was finding the adjustment rather tough. I didn't like the adjustment at all. It was difficult for me. However, In my sophomore year of High school, I realized that my parents were doing everything they could to make sure I would make it. They wanted me to make it, and I didn't know at that time that everything they did would pay off. Let me be honest with you, the most difficulty years by far were the early adolescent years. Transitioning to middle school, I took a nose dive with my education. What was once A's became F's. I didn't care at this point about school. I saw it as a waste of time. I remember coming home one day and telling Mom and Dad at dinner that I didn't care about my education anymore, and that I wasn't going to school. Dad looked at me and responded with the sarcastic response: " Oh really? That's interesting you say that. So tell me how that's going to work out for you? You see son, school is important. As long as you live in my house you'll be in school."

I wasn't a huge fan of the wisdom and parenting knowledge at the time, but looking back, I would tell younger Finn he needed to whip it into shape, because life is what you make it. Choose to make good choices and life will be easy. If not, life is hard. That is one of my dads famous lines. When I was about 15 years old that quote made sense to me.

By this time I was fourteen years old, I finally had a grasp on my education, I understood my life was important, but I still didn't really love, or care about anything or anyone. In the early developmental stages of writing this chapter, I prayed about sharing bits and pieces of my story, especially the vulnerable bits. The year 2012 holds a very significant drop pin in my life. After fourteen years of living in my own isolation, not wanting to trust, to love, to receive love, always angry, bullying, disobeying, mistreating people, behaving rebelliously, and choosing to live a cold and difficult life, I surrendered my life to Jesus on New Year's Eve when I had my encounter with the Lord. I spent thirty minutes writing my New Year's resolutions as a way to start my year doing better. However, when I had my encounter, my resolutions turned into a deep complex and emotional prayer. I wasn't a super religious person. As a matter of fact I didn't really find any interest in the whole relationship with God, going to church and praying. Well, this was by far one of the most memorable moments of my life. It's so crazy because I remember this like it was yesterday. I remember writing down a few things I would do differently, my goals for school, How was going to be kinder etc. It was like a transition in a Movie. I went from writing down the bullet points to writing a letter in the form of a prayer. Within this prayer, I began to write a letter in which I had asked God for forgiveness. I went on to write about the life I wanted, to forgive and love my parents, and that I was tired of living my life in such a hot mess.

In a later chapter, I will elaborate more about the encounter that changed my life. People have asked me what motivated me to change and to live my life for Christ. It's one of those things you can try to explain to people, but honestly, It's like describing the taste of a strawberry, everyone's experience is different. My relationship with the Lord has been a foundational aspect of my personal and spiritual growth. Over the years I became more and more aware of what my purpose is and how my ministry will reach thousands. One thing I point out to people when I share my story or coach them on a specific area that I can relate to is that not everyone will understand the relationship with Jesus. Since 2012, my life has not been the same. As a matter of fact, each day I thank the Lord for saving me from the fear I was dealing with. When I first hit the ground, I started to cry. In that moment though, I felt my pain, anger, rejection, and fear lift off my body as if someone took a sixty pound backpack off my shoulders. I can attest that my childhood was not a walk in the park for either my parents or me. However, God knew that I would overcome and restore what may have been lost, or broken. Many of us look back and want to change things, and I see why people would. However even with how my life had been at the time, without the struggles, without the detours, I would not have made it to where I am today. The thrill of growth is that uncomfortable feeling. We all experience it, but being content in a seated position would eventually become uncomfortable and you would more than likely get up and adjust.

For me personally, God has provided a "road trip": this walk I am taking called life. It has been filled with its ups and downs, detours, and setbacks, and with every direction imaginable it pushed me to learn more and more about me.

I recall a time I sat down with a group of young adults at a camp retreat and we gathered in the Pow Wow circle. One of the young adults asked me why didn't God just get rid of the enemy completely when he shunned him from heaven? I chuckled, and said that's a great question.

I pondered for a bit, and found some words to answer his question. God isn't going to force us to love, or have a relationship with him. But he certainly gives us the opportunity to choose him, his kingdom and to love all people, in all places, at all times. All too many times we paint this image of God as a man who sits on a throne and shakes his head all day at the silly things we do. The truth is that God is after you and I no matter the bruises, no matter the hurt, no matter the pain or how deep the wound is, He truly loves us.

There is a song by Christian musician; TobyMac called Backseat Driver. The focal point of the song is that TobyMac looks to God to navigate him through his life and to be the driver of his life. We tend to go back to our old ways, but instead would rather be in the backseat seeing where God is taking him. At one point in my life I thought I was the driver, but I was getting tired of driving nowhere but into ditches. Therefore, I surrender my life and Jesus took the wheel. Folks, I want you to know that the choices we make, and the encounters we have today, are going to determine how tomorrow will be. I may be young, and writing a book was something at one point I did not have cross my mind. Did I mention I never enjoyed English and Language Arts classes? Throughout this book, I share different encounters I have had. How each encounter had such a significance in my life. Each part of the way changed me for the purpose I'm called for and that I am thankful for. Being adopted is a blessing. Mom and Dad never gave up on me. They may not have understood everything at the time, but God gave them the strength, unconditional love, and guidance to navigate through the journey.

Chapter 2 | Embrace the Experience

When I was eighteen, I had reached a milestone in my life. I had gone through my high school years learning academics as well as diving into the word of God daily. Learning to become an independent adult was one of the most uncomfortable situations I had to overcome. In order to step up in life, you will face the moments you have to step back as well. Stepping back isn't necessarily a bad thing, it's an opportunity for us to mend pieces together that may need work. I do my best to encourage people to become aware that each of us have the rest of our life to choose the life we want to have. Consequences or rewards will result, but don't forget that you ultimately can change your course to become the best version of yourself. Learning that you choose how you recover will make life that much easier. Some of us are not ready to accept this fact, but I hope as you read on, knowing a bit more about who I am and what I was dealing with, you will come to realize that no matter your circumstance you can find peace and comfort with life when you are ready to. I have never expected any person that I've come in contact with to feel that they have be a Christ follower to talk to me, or engage with me. Complete opposite actually. I intentionally wrote this book for people of all walks of life. At one point in my life I didn't have a relationship with Jesus, nor did I want one. Then again, here I am writing a book, sharing vulnerable parts of my life with you, hosting a motivational podcast, reaching people globally, and constantly serving within my community to encourage people I encounter. Throughout this book, I hope you are finding moments to pick up what I am laying down. Taking the steps to become better at being you takes courage, trust, and faith. I know that it can be misleading and difficult at times. I am hoping that you are reading with a sense of ease and confidence so that you can be more clear minded, focused, and even courageous to face the day-to-day obstacles, your constant insecurities, and so forth. Some of us like to read to be challenged, or to be educated. Some of you reading this might be in a season in your life at the moment in which you are not sure how to step forward. Maybe you are not too sure how to reach your next goal or aspiration.

The world is constantly changing; people are getting smarter, technology is becoming more user-friendly, cars are becoming more efficient. With change happening so frequently and so rapidly, we must become more equipped to adapt. Each day as the sun begins to warm the face of the earth, people in Hong Kong, Paris, New York, just to mention a few, are doing what we all learn from the time we are children, and that is practicing a daily routine. This "common practice" we all know is called *habit*. I have revised this book on multiple occasions, and I often find that I need to add more. Sometimes I will reread a chapter contemplating if I need to add more or take some out. I had multiple visions when I first starting writing. First of all, each of you will have the opportunity to learn the spiritual, emotional, mental, psychological, and even physical perspective of what it's like to be YOU so that you can gain knowledge of the basic fundamentals, principles, and processes of life.

It is important to take time for you. I promote self-care because it is a vital part of growth. With this being said, I highly encourage you to give yourself some time to really focus on *you*. Find how each of these different fundamentals are helping you develop habits and a routine to balance your life, family, work, and, most importantly, YOU. On another note, do yourself a favor and be patient with yourself so that you can honestly and thoroughly receive the full message of this book. There are moments when I wrote this book I wasn't sure how I was going to deliver my story. It was a struggle finding a place to even start. I tried my best to write this book as if I was talking to you. Ideally, making it more personal because I believe in connecting with people. This is the beautiful part of being an author: making an effort to connect with your reader in an almost seamless open dialogue. Obviously you are reading, but I am sure when you have read a book you make connections with the author and what they want you to receive. I have always been one to go against the grain. When people said I couldn't, I said I could. When people said there was no way, I said there was a way.

Lastly, I urge that you stay positive and focus on growing. I run into many people who have their dreams and goals lined up but fail to execute. What stopped you? I want to help you revive those dream that you tucked away. Many of us tuck these dreams away in a box and don't plan on revisiting them However, If anyone is going to tell you let it be me. Those dreams make your story. It's part of your color pallet. I encourage you to not neglect your dreams, rather embrace them and make them happen. Honestly, learn to listen to all, but sift through what is going to propel you forward in life. I'll share with you that many people questioned my capacity of experience to write a book. I can understand why they would. I'm young, and what do I have to share? Well not to be cliché, but you can't judge a book by its cover. My intention for this book is to share my journey with you, hoping that it will empower you so that no matter what part of life you are experiencing, it will reignite your flame. We have all experienced something throughout our lives that may have positively or negatively impacted us in becoming the person we are today.

When I was fourteen years old, I had just started my freshman year of high school. If you recall I wasn't all too enthusiastic about my education in middle school, however I had changed my outlook on my education after sixth grade. I remember I used to complain to my dad about how hard and unfair life was. Now that I look back on it, Life was only tough because I made it tough.

I remember coming home one afternoon, complaining about some homework assignment as I marched to my room with a poopy attitude. Dad had followed and suggested I'd write a book about how unfair my life was. I looked at him and thought he was joking. He wasn't. I think he was pretty serious actually. I used to think he was crazy when he said write a book. I had no interest in writing a book at the time. It is funny because the name of the book was going to be *The Unfair Life of Finn*. I'm glad that book never really became of anything. I realized later on Dad was just trying to utilize the concept of writing a book as a way to journal about it instead of talking about, but as a seventh grader writing a book seemed overwhelming. To be honest I was overwhelmed on multiple occasions writing this book. Over the years, I came to a realization that I had to grow, discover, and become comfortable with change. I wasn't ready to commit to change and growth at the time. When I was about 16 years old, I started understanding what Dad was trying to teach me. It wasn't anything complicated; it was very basic and this is how he would phrase it: "Making good choices makes life easy. Making bad choices makes life hard." To this day we still talk about those lessons he wanted me to learn, he simply just says you weren't ready. You can't force a plant to grow, and you can't make a butterfly fly. One must go through a process, sometimes it takes longer to learn, but the hopes is eventually to break free. I know that in life sometimes it just seems like everything is coming down on you. We have those moments where we feel life is hard and unfair, but I don't expect you to write a book. I continue to pray that this book empowers you to recognize that you have the potential to be who you want to be, the potential to do what you want to do, and the potential to live your life with a cultivated mindset to make growth, success, and opportunities routine and not occasional. One thing I may be a bit biased about are the Life Hack books. I don't think there is one right way of doing life, we all contribute to the melting pot of experiences but no one way is more perfect than the next. However, I will point out that setting a high demanding goal or expectation can set your reader up to potentially lose focus, grit and even a sense of confidence in who they are. It is crucial that we set realistic and achievable goals that may be short term. Setting multiple short term goals will progressively get you closer to your major goal more effectively and along the way you build the confidence and endurance to maximize your life. I wrote this book to connect with you on a level that will provide a sturdy and easy to read biographical and motivational book that doesn't require anything but yourself, some time, and some grit. I always believed that an author who is willing to share deeper parts of their life, will connect with his audience a lot more securely.

Some of you may take this as reassurance that even those who struggle will be OK. Some of you may take this as an opportunity to learn, grow, adapt, and revolutionize your life. Some people are simply not ready to make the step in the direction they want to go. And that is OK. That is why I encourage you to continue to read. No one can rush you, force you, or make you if you don't want to make the step, but giving people the opportunity to change or want to make a better choice is acceptable. Remember, this book is for people of all walks in life. I believe anyone can take away something for themselves from this book. It is not a race to see who will be better or who is more abundant in their endeavors. As a matter of fact, this is a lot like a marathon. We run together, but the goal to the finish isn't against the other runners, it's YOU. We all have our struggles, setbacks, and opportunities, so what may seem more or less great to you may very well be amazing for someone else. It's not always easy to change your ways and do things a bit differently. We all like to be comfortable and apply our own spice to life, but it is good once in a while to let someone suggest a more user-friendly way to live so you can save your well-being over a lifetime, not temporarily. I love listening to people who have a story. And guess who has a story? EVERYONE! We all have a story to tell. We all are connected, and we all are capable of making the steps to become who we want to become.

I'm not going to say it's easy, but I hope this book allows you to understand and be encouraged that taking the step to grow, discover, and learn about yourself has a huge reward to include more prosperity, more abundance, breakthroughs, comfort, and familiarity with living life the way you want. As I've already mentioned, this may not be easy; however, it will be doable, and I have faith that you and those that read *This Is Me* will do great things. Keep in mind as you begin this new chapter in life, that with change comes learning. I was once told in Basic Military Training, that being comfortable uncomfortable is half the battle. We are programmed to adjust and adapt, which is a beautiful lesson we learn as life goes on!

Chapter 3 | Mountains + Valleys

I often find myself relating mountains and valleys to our struggles and our successes throughout life. Throughout the past few years, I have had to remind myself and others that in life we will find ourselves in a valley or at some point on top of a mountain. I just recently went on a trip to Georgia to visit my friends for the weekend and while there I spent some time focusing on this chapter of the book. I started my road trip with some Instagram Live action as always and maximizing my opportunity to reach someone with motivation. I spent quite a bit of time sightseeing, wandering, and gathering my thoughts and intentions for this chapter. Something that I took away from writing this chapter was that when you spend time with yourself, and really evaluate who you are, you truly get to know yourself a whole lot better. No matter if you are struggling, or if things are just peachy, you have to take a hike in life, and soon enough you will look down into the valley you once stood in and smile because YOU accomplished, overcame, broke through your situation. Not to mention this cycle of valleys and mountains is part of life, so don't be intimidated by the elevation of your hike; just know each moment you encounter, God is preparing you for the next hike in your life. I continue to pray that this book brings motivation and encouragement as you now have reached another checkpoint.

Over the past several months, I have connected with so many people on a level that has helped others and even myself grow. In my motivational discussions, our podcast, and doing RealTalks, an Instagram Live Series started in 2021, I focus on rekindling the importance of becoming the best version of you. Helping people create routine, cultivate a mindset to overcome, empower people to confront their insecurities, this is what I live for. I try my best to remind younger adults that elevation, growth, and availability, will help you become the best version of yourself, and truly learn to love yourself. The Bible says to love your neighbor as yourself. In order for you to embrace others and love others, it all starts with you. My dad would use the example of the oxygen levels pressure in the airplane cabin and the O2 masks dropping down as an example. Last I recalled the flight attendant inform the passengers per the safety guidelines, In case the oxygen levels change in the cabin, to put your mask on securely before assisting the person beside you with theirs.

In order for you to take care of someone else, you must learn to take care of yourself first. You gain knowledge and experience so that you can help elevate someone you may come across. Something I have recently been working on with young adults was becoming aware of the "uncomfortable." Sometimes we are not aware of what is happening, what to do, or how to cope in situations that create fear, confusion, or maybe even loneliness.

However, as I find more and more reason to help people, I try and connect real world concepts to coach and encourage people to embrace a package that contains struggle and success: It's called LIFE. Embrace the valleys and mountains you will encounter, because the only way to reach the top is to make the choice to climb. A popular set of questions that I commonly get from people is, "Why do I experience good and bad moments? Why do I struggle sometimes? Will I ever get out of this valley?" Instead of asking Why, I encourage people to ask these questions differently. What can I do to maximize the good and bad moments? What can I do to be more successful? Learning to ask what instead of why promotes self-reflection instead of self-infliction. When we ask why, we tend to embed blame and guilt and the response leads to guilt, doubt, and insecurities.

One important factor to go ahead and implement is that no matter how much you want to avoid it, struggle is a process. Often we want to bypass struggle not realizing that struggle is the part of the journey that humbles us, makes us stronger, and gives us a reason to push past our limits I recently got back into the gym and found that I gained a significant amount of weight. I would ask myself what are you going to do to get back into shape? Staring in the mirror wasn't going to change anything. So I started back in the gym. I had saw they changes my body took and I needed to do something about it. It all starts with a motivation. Regardless of the amount of motivation I had, I still needed to work out because if you don't go through the process, your body won't build muscle. You have to condition your body, right? Imagine this with life. You set a goal, maybe nursing school, and then you put in the work for the two to four years you study. Most of my nursing friends have told me that you will be sacrificing your free time. But the reward at the end is worth it. I don't ever want people to feel ashamed that they are struggling, or feel as if they can't overcome. I know because I remember I had moments I felt that I would never overcome my fear, anger, or even the simple fact that life always seemed to be against me.

Successful people didn't make it to where they are today because someone did it for them. Elon Musk, CEO of Tesla and Space X, woke up one day and said I want to develop a vehicle that runs on solely electricity, send a rocket to space and set the record for the wealthiest and successful entrepreneur in the world. And so he did. He struggled along the way, but because of his consistency and failing enough times to succeed he has created an impact around the globe. Steve Jobs and Simon Sinek, to mention just a few others, had to face struggle in their lives, but because they were willing to face the struggle, they were able to impact and elevate people. If you notice the pattern here, people who have a story, have impacted people in one way or another. Throughout my life, I have found myself in a valley, and even trapped myself into thinking I will never get out of this circumstance. Truth is, I was stuck at times because I created my initial thoughts from my fear, worry, and not being rational about the obstacles I had before me. I want you to think about a valley you may have had, or maybe you are currently in. I want to remind you that this is not necessarily a bad place, but just a moment in which you get to self-critique and reflect a little. Many of us want life to have bowling bumper rails up to prevent us from encountering struggle. We fear that we won't make it to the top, or that we can't elevate to our next season.

One of my best friends and co-host on the podcast *The Best You Nation*, Adler, is one of the most motivational and God-fearing men I know. Adler and I share a common passion and drive to coach people so they can manage their drive, optimize the 24 hours we have in a day and ultimately become the best version of themselves. Adler has a way of being creative with how he explains things. Adler has faced many obstacles in his life, and now joins me on a podcast weekly to speak on topics that people want to listen to. Adler once reminded me that we may be in a season of struggle, or maybe we are in a season of promotion, elevation, and success. Either way, God orchestrates our journey for us, and we can't change that. We need God, and He knows our plans better than you and I do. Proverbs 16:9 says, "In their hearts humans plan their course, but the Lord establishes their steps." He made us, and He knows what you are capable of doing.

I like using the example of the bike I bought at Walmart. At Walmart, some bikes are not complete and are still in the box wrapped up ready for you to buy. I bought a bike, and I went ahead and began to assemble it according to how I thought it was supposed to be put together. I failed to use the instruction manual that was included. About an hour later, feeling great about my bike, I went ahead and took it for a spin. Within seconds it fell apart and a wheel rolled off due to a nut not being properly screwed on. I know this may seem like a simple fix, or just a small issue, but the reality is that sometimes in life we do the same thing. We want to tackle our obstacle (bike) and not use our instruction manual (Bible) to accomplish this task.

The manufacturer of the bike knows the bike better than we do, and so therefore in relation, God (manufacturer) knows me and my life (bike) better too. Everyone struggles, and some of you might be struggling right now. However, I'm here to tell you how you can overcome and tackle this obstacle and you don't even have to pack heavy, just make sure you have yourself, and a smile, to take with you on this hike. That's right, no big secret; just a simple concept that will help you reach your mountain, and anytime you feel stuck in your valley, you will be equipped like a pro! I mentioned my trip to Georgia, and the alone time I had while I was there. I had the opportunity to love myself and spend time with myself to honestly learn about myself. Well, I also spent a tremendous amount of time with friends and new friends hiking early mornings, going through a corn maze, and catching a spin at the fair. Therefore, I want you to join me as we go on our "hike," in which I will use some of the real life obstacles I had on our sunrise hike to paint an image for you so you can find the connection point.

First of all, I want to remind you how awesome you are! I am beyond proud of you, and I'm only hoping this book is giving you insight of how we can be better at who we are one day at a time. I know there are a lot of books in this world, but I believe each book will impact and give someone the opportunity to maximize their life in a personalized way. Whatever it is that you are finding to touch your heart, I hope it will forever keep you elevated. But hey, you and I have a "hike" to accomplish. I hope your bag is packed and you have all that you need. Let's get hiking!

You may have had a struggle that seemed a bit daunting in your life. Possibly you are one reader of many that is going through something right now. At the bottom of some of our mountains, we find financial burdens, toxic relationships, family issues, marital disputes, school, stress, personal obstacles, lack of motivation, depression, anxiety, abuse, even addiction. You look at it and you may have been intimidated by it, but you are trying to break free from it. As you begin to recognize and analyze your situation, you continue to want a way out, find peace, find a breakthrough. There really is no other way to get to your breakthrough point but taking steps to reach the top of this mountain. I always remind people that you have a choice. I can motivate, elevate, encourage; however, if you don't make the ultimate decision to change, or take a hike, you will continue to sit in your valley. With every hike, there is always some sort of challenge that you may come across such as the fear of the trail being small, big rocks in the way, the critters along the way, maybe even the elevation can be a bit overwhelming. These overwhelming things can sometimes slow us down to get to the top. I have even brought to light that sometimes we keep ourselves from reaching the top. However, I want to help people break from that!

As we continue to move along the trail, we have come across big rocks that we may trip over, steep slopes along the trail giving us very little space to walk, and it's still dark outside since it's still early in the morning. Remember we are striving to seeing our "sunset"; or in this case, our breakthrough is what we are striving to see!

In life, sometimes we find that "hiking" can be scary, too much, or even tiring. I am sure we have all begun to question ourselves: Can I do it? Will I make it to the top? How far do I have to go? I have asked myself these questions many times. I recall the times that just the distance was discouraging and I didn't want to go on the "hike." I have also been discouraged, finding that I couldn't find any change or improvement if I took a hike. Many of you may have the same questions, feelings of discouragement, or even lack of motivation to try. I encourage you to trust that even when the path seems bumpy, rocky, narrow, or even just long, trust that you are capable of making it as it is rewarding to make it to the top. We have encountered some rocky patches of the trail and an increase in elevation, which makes it a bit harder and also maybe more physically demanding. Well, don't stop, because this is where it gets good. You may have heard your PE coach or even trainer tell you, "No pain, no gain." No one said it was going to be easy! It's definitely doable, but you have to push through and keep your chin up. Sometimes we give up on a routine of pushups at the gym because they hurt. Maybe you give up on a task at work because you feel overwhelmed. If it was easy, then it wouldn't make for a feel-good feeling when you accomplished something or overcame with a breakthrough. I hope by now as we continue to strive for the top of the mountain, your legs are feeling a bit stronger, and you still have your chin up for a success story that will go into your book! Many of us have to keep some form of motivation in our minds, hearts, and even sight. Each and every one of you has something that keeps you going, and I want you to keep that in mind as we approach the top. I also want to share with you that sometimes on your hike in life, we want to take shortcuts. Everyone, including me, likes a good shortcut. However, when it comes to life, shortcuts can lead to hazard and may not be good for us. Just because there might be a shorter path, doesn't mean that it is the best.

I don't know anyone who's ever started their hike from the top of the mountain first. You may notice that change or growth doesn't happen overnight. I know that sounds good, but to be honest sometimes it's not until a few steps (realistically a few days, a few weeks, even a few months) that you truly are 100 percent motivated and learning to be comfortable even when it seems impossible. This is probably the most important part to take away at this point.

Your journey/hike is what disciplines, builds strength and endurance, to get you to your breakthrough point. Therefore, the final stretch to the end of our hike, we focus on the goal more and more.

It's a natural reaction to be anxious, excited, and proud to reach the top. Yes! This is the energy I would hope you find as you overcome your obstacles. Anytime I find myself in a situation where I worry, stress, or wonder if I can get through this, I begin to look for my motive, and begin to hike. Sometimes it takes a long time to overcome a situation such as a toxic relationship, student debt, or negative personal decisions.

However, when you see change, and you've learned to adapt to being comfortable being uncomfortable, then you've only gotten that much closer to the top of your mountain. We are finally reaching the top, and we are sweating, and maybe even a bit thirsty. Metaphorically speaking, I'm sure you want to sit and take a break.

Sometimes we get close to the top and after all the hard work, and overcoming, we convince ourselves that we are done. Don't allow yourself to be convinced that you are done if you still have a little ways to go.

I tell you this because many people will struggle with something and begin working to get better, but as they reach the end, they crash and burn to the fear of false hope and dissatisfaction, even though they knew there is a positive result called a breakthrough. I strongly suggest that anytime you feel that you can't finish or you don't have the motivation, remind yourself that you've come this far, and remember your "why." Struggling moments are times where most of us are vulnerable. Where most of us don't really understand what the reason is for being here. Continue to analyze, and apply your positive thoughts so that you can continue to reach for your breakthrough point. Just food for thought: as I get older I find myself realizing that the further and further on I go with my hike, it's a little bit harder than the last hike. It doesn't mean it's not doable; it just means it requires a little bit more motivation, concentration, more discipline, and focus. Realizing where we are in life is sometimes one of the most difficult struggles we face. We want to be on the right track, we want to make sure everything is right and because we don't always realize what we are we doing, it could be adding or taking away from our daily grind.

Sometimes in your struggling moments you are not going to understand "why," and you and I both need to accept that. Many of us want instant gratification, we want it right now, we want to know it right now. However, if life was based on instant gratification, we wouldn't learn right from wrong, we wouldn't understand how life works, and ultimately we wouldn't know how to be us. My personal belief is that God is teaching us to become better throughout our journey, and with every hike you take, you learn a little more. He doesn't find humor in our struggles, he only wants to make sure you and I have the knowledge that life isn't about instant gratification. Rather, it's about having patience and taking your time to become better at being YOU.

I took the time to write a book because I felt led to motivate and elevate people so they can be reminded that no matter what walk in life we are on, each of us is capable of doing anything and everything we want. But I want people to remember that when you go back and think about your mountains, think about your valleys too, and what made you want to go climb and overcome. Because when we reach the top, sometimes we forget where we started. Remember struggle is the process, and success is the result. When I really started walking in my purpose, I saw the potential in so many people.

God began to reveal the hurts, doubts, and potential in people that I came in contact with. Everybody comes from a different walk and I respect what people believe. I respect what people think. I respect people's opinions. I hope for the same when I tell you that I promise you that as I continue to step forth in the direction that God is calling me to go, the more and more that I see him doing things for his people, the more I start seeing what God is calling me to do, I simply want to elevate people and share my passion for life, love, and joy. God doesn't allow you and me to struggle because he's bored. God allows us to struggle because it's encouraging us to become the better version of ourselves. Keep climbing!

Chapter 4 | The Encounter

I am excited about this chapter, and its purpose for you and other readers. Many of us live our lives determined, inspired, and motivated to make choices that are creating opportunities for us to strive for greatness. In this chapter I'd like to focus on a few things that will help you understand how to live out the best encounter in life. Each of you have your own exclusive "encounter," but we can revisit how each of us got to this point. My best encounter in life was giving myself to Christ and making an effort to change not only myself but to guide other people to Jesus as well. Starting up a youth group a few years ago and focusing on helping younger adults become closer to God has been humbling and rewarding. Each day you will find yourself learning more about yourself, becoming comfortable with struggles, and understanding some days are going to be better than other, However, you have everything within reach to choose to live the life you want to live. If God has intended for you to be where he wants you to be, appreciate those moments, be reminded that he knows best, and make choices that get you closer to him. In this chapter you'll find the best lessons life are the ones that have the greatest impact on us. Some of you may have given your life to Christ, some of you may have moved in the direction in which you want to grow in your company that you work for, or maybe it's as simple as overcoming some of the debts in life. Don't worry, we are all here to learn what it's like to live in one motion; therefore, this chapter is dedicated to your best life decision that has impacted you to continue to push for the greater things in your life even if it is not clear to you at the moment.

When I was younger, I didn't necessarily have an exclusive relationship with Jesus. I would go to church, but not engage in fellowship. Fourteen years of my twenty-three years of life, I lived in my own shadow of anger, upset, fear, and uncertainty. If you recall from Chapter 3 your valleys are those individual moments in which a struggle is more like a current event where you may be at your lowest or most vulnerable. I didn't necessarily understand why I was choosing to make the choices I was making, why I was rebellious against my parents, why I chose to be so mean and disrespectful to not only my peers but also those around me on a daily basis.

Sometimes we find ourselves stuck, we find ourselves being in places where we don't necessarily want to be, but how do we understand why we are where we are? At some point in your life, you've made a decision where you wanted to do something better for yourself, and that my friends is amazing! I amend you for that! Some people struggle to recognize that part of the growth process. By now, you may have figured out the encounter that I speak of is the time I gave my life to Christ. I revealed that my relationship with Jesus is not just a relationship, it's not just a wake up every day and pray and go to church kind of thing, it's a foundational aspect of my life. Prior to my relationship with Christ, I didn't have any ambition to acknowledge his walk here on earth. The importance of this chapter is to highlight the pivoting point of life. You may recall that a large percentage of children who are adopted, have a significantly harder time developing social skills, personal relationships, and a motive to live a good life. For some people who may read this may not understand the relationship aspect, and that's okay. I'm not here to judge, simply express that this part of my life gave me hope beyond what I already had before me.

Sit back for a second and think about where you may just be in your life. Breathe in and Breathe out for a just a second. Become aware of where you are and what you doing. I want you think about what kind of environment you live in. For example, if you live in Orlando, you would consider yourself living in a large city. Just take this moment to acknowledge where you are. What you call home. Now imagine you are in an environment where you are not so familiar. For example, My friends who live in a cooler climate, imagine being in Florida. Of course I am sure you would appreciate the warmth, however it is an adjustment to get used to here in Florida. My point that I am making is simple. Adapting and facing the moments that make us uncomfortable. You and I have to learn to become more aware of not only our opportunities, but the places that we are supposed to go, the people we meet, and the impact we make on each other. When I gave my life to Christ, I saw myself growing and learning in a different perspective. I was sitting on the back porch of my pastor's house on New Year's Eve, writing my resolutions and goals for the new year.

I jotted down the typical: no chocolate, working out, getting fit, being nice to people, staying in shape, and so on. Within thirty minutes of coming up with my resolutions, I got to a point where I started writing down a prayer that became more and more personal. I then could hear a clear voice calling my name. I thought I was just hearing things. It was somewhat faint but I could hear it, and I kept thinking it was my pastor yelling from the front yard. Over and over again I kept hearing my name being shouted. Yet again it wasn't my pastor. Now at this point I was really confused, and thinking I was losing it. It became very clear. Almost like he was sitting down right next to me. It was as simple as, "Are you listening to me? Why are you not looking for me? I love you!" These are just a few words I could vividly make out when I was sitting there. The weird part of this is that it was very cold outside, but my body was very warm even though I was wearing a T-shirt and gym shorts. The presence of the Lord was strong and noticeable. At that point I knew that there was something else much greater than my resolution session. It was incredible. I wrote down Bible verses that I'd never read, Bible scripture that applied to me, highlighting parts of the Bible that to this day I refer to. This was the best encounter of my life. It was a foundational moment for me. Jesus is my rock, He takes me from left to right, He lifts me up when I'm down, He takes me from every direction that He needs to take me, and some of us just don't understand that part of our life story. Each day I strive to live, love, and unite with others to elevate others for the glory of God. God has created diversity and unity for us to come together and to love each other. Not only to just sit together, or to enjoy coffee together, but to actually get together and fellowship in His name. Your encounter is something nobody can tell you to do, ask you to do, force you to do. It is simply getting up one day, getting out, getting ready for what you will face today.

I finally had the time and motivation to write a book to share a motivational memoir and share my movement to fellowship, uniting His people under his one love, his one mission, and his one son. People don't believe in struggling, people don't believe in consequences. People believe that life is handed to them on a silver platter, and unfortunately that is not how it works. If it was easy, there would be no purpose in life, no motivation to strive, and no reason for living out each day for Him.

You may have to ask yourself multiple times where you want to be in five years, maybe even looking yourself in the mirror and saying, "Well, this is what I can do, this is how I can get there." Write yourself some sticky notes and place them on your mirror to remind yourself that you are a creation of God and that you have a choice to live each day to the fullest.

At some point in my life, I finally chose to write a book. It didn't come easy. Multiple times I wanted to make it happen, but I couldn't get started or find the motivation to do so. It took three years of prayer, a multiple come-to-Jesus moments, and a goal to publish 2021. Some of us are convinced that the ideas that we have, the things that we believe in, are not good enough or aren't valid. *Stop!* You are you, and nobody can change that. God has created us in his perfect image, and I am sure he didn't make a mistake when he made you and I. God allows us to go through certain things, at certain times of our life, so that we can better not only ourselves but even other people around us. Our personal experiences in life shape us to be who we are. Some may go more south than north with them, but eventually we will face Jesus. Remember Jesus was in the valley for forty days and forty nights. He was tempted, he was given opportunities to fall for what the enemy wanted him to fall for; however, the Son of God was not going to allow him to win. Have resilience like JC!

First Corinthians chapter 12 talks about diversity and thoroughly explains why God created us the way we are. Each and every one of us have our own unique gifts. We each have to come together to unite in one love, one family, and one faith. John 17:22 specifically emphasizes the prayer that Jesus prayed to his father in the garden. The message that should be received is the unification of Jesus and God, as well as the unification of the people. Too many of us walk away from or lose focus on what the mission or the purpose for our life is.

Therefore, sometimes we just need a little reminder that we can live each day knowing that God created us to be diverse and loved, and to live for His will be done. There are 7 billion people in the world and not everyone is going to agree, or understand what may make sense to us individually. Living in one motion is all about knowing to take it day by day, each step at a time. It's just like walking, you land your left foot down then land your right foot down and repeat. Embrace your encounter. You will see that as you begin to reach others, you will have the opportunity to elevate someone to reach their encounter. Be

encouraged that in every season of your life, there is a
purpose for you. It all comes down to knowing what you
are called to do on this earth. #KeepEmbracing

Chapter 5 | The Dash in Between

When I was younger, I had the opportunity to attend a leadership camp with the CVJM, which was a Christian youth group organization I was a part of while living in Munster, Germany. Each year all regions of the CVJM would take three major trips to include spring, summer, and fall camps. During the 2007 fall camp, the younger guys in our group had an exclusive opportunity to attend a leadership class held offsite from the campgrounds. It was about halfway through the week that this leadership class was held at most camps, but the younger guys usually didn't attend. One morning, we were woken early, got ready, ate breakfast, and got on the bus to leave camp for the day. Most of the time the young guys would be preoccupied with camp duties such as clean-up crew, making sure the campsite was clean, and once we were done, we would go swimming in the creek, fellowship, work on our skits for the evening bonfire. However, this was an exclusive opportunity that we had. After about an hour of driving, we finally arrived at what had looked like an old ramshackle sign that said "Begin Here" in German. Most leadership classes we know of wouldn't be a hike in the Black Forest, but this was definitely unique. Our leader gave us clear direction as to keep each other accountable, told us not to pick any berries, and made sure we traveled as a group.

We began to hike along the trail into the mountains as our leader began to sing our Camp Song. By the time he finished the first verse, the whole group was singing along too! We had been traveling for some time, and many of us young guys were wondering where we were headed. Don't get me wrong, I enjoy hiking and venturing into the mountains, but what did this hike have to do with leadership? Life? Anything really? We came upon an old graveyard near a small village not far from where we would continue. Our leader stopped and took a moment to explain the significance of the graveyard. He then went on about the date that was written on the tombstone and that most people acknowledge the years but not the DASH.

I honestly had never really thought about the dash in between the year someone was born and the year they passed. It was then that our leader began to elaborate more about the dash and why so many of us don't see it any more than just the dash in between the two years. The purpose of this short story is to open your eyes to knowing the importance of the dash. Many of us just see it and say, "Wow, that person lived a long time," without giving any thought on what that person may have done in their life, accomplished, failed, re-learned, and the whole nine yards. My point is, that dash is more than a small line, it's more than just a separation between two different years. It marks a legacy of an individual.

I'll never forget that class, nor will I forget the importance of the dash. Too many of us live life as if we have forever to accomplish things, meet our significant other, graduate college, and launch a career. For some it's even starting a family, or launching a business. So the question we should be asking ourselves, if we are truly honest with ourselves, is, "How long will I wait until I start living and making the most of my dreams, goals, and gifts God has put inside of me?" Every season of life, every year that we live, every moment we encounter, it all has value. I knew at some point in my life I needed a starting point. Somewhere to begin. For five short years I had lived my life with no sense of direction, really not focused on my life as I should have been, with absolutely no intention of ever really working, or even graduating. Many of us have seen or been in a place where we have drifted far, lost sight of our purpose, and maybe even lost motivation, yet we are content with how life was at the time. If I can be honest with you, there was no easy route to change, forgiveness, humility, confidence, overcoming, joy, and all other aspects of life we each experience. I am almost confident nobody goes looking for struggle or failure in their life. Nobody asks for a handout of unfortunate circumstances, and encounters that may raise doubt and fear. However, we have to recall that we are living in the DASH. I share with people all the time that we can't bypass struggle. I used to think there was an easy route through life. But truthfully there is no easy or hard way through life. It all comes down to how your respond to the situations you and I face, as well as the end goal you have in mind. God has given us a timeline on earth, and we must live each moment to the fullest even when it seems to be a season of difficulty.

Furthermore, you and I have to answer the question: How do we really start living our best life? I want you to take a moment and ask yourself this question a good five times, and maybe even scribble it down on a sticky note so you don't forget. I like sticky notes because they are easy to use, and I like organizing them on my wall so I can remember them. Each sticky basically represents a thought, question, or comment I have for myself, God, or even someone I might run into by chance. I always encourage people to find what makes organizing their thoughts easiest and stick to it! So, now with us both having to answer this question, here are my thoughts and response for you. Too many times in my life I would give up when I couldn't master a task. I would convince myself that it was easier to never try it, then keep trying. Over the years, I had learned this brilliant concept inspired by a professor at Ohio State, Brian Kite, who taught his students this basic formula: E+R=O. It basically means: Events + Reaction = Outcome, which goes for both positive and negative outcomes/encounters. I find it important to understand that in order to live your best life, to accomplish everything you want to accomplish, to meet all your goals and ambitions, you really need to know the mind, body and spirit aspect so you can optimize your life to the maximum. God created us uniquely and designed us to rationalize, identify, and respond.

One of my favorite memories as a child was riding bikes with my brother. We'd ride bikes for hours at a time. We would ride down the forbidden paths, cut corners, and make turns where we weren't so sure the path would lead us. As a kid, you wouldn't think about the life lesson in taking the not so sure path versus a path we were familiar with. My brother and I had to choose the path we rode our bikes on, whether it be the one with all the bumps and detours, or the path that would keep us focused and allowed us to wander and explore.

A lot of the time we encounter similar paths like the ones I described above. The path that we choose, whether it be the path of wisdom or the path of foolishness, this will be the manifestation of the progress in our purpose. Your purpose is not your destination, it is your journey. Too many times I have heard people saying, "I can't wait to get to next year." or something like, "This year is OK, but I am hoping next year is even better." It is great to hope and want the best, but in order to reach such great heights, you must identify the *right now*. The moment you neglect the current moment is the moment you reach a halt in progress. Often, we are more interested in the destination, which is wonderful. However, the view and experiences along the way give us the opportunity to appreciate the destination versus just proclaiming " I have reached the top". There is a sense of purpose, and reward when we have to work our way to the top. Remember back to the Mountains and Valleys, the in between the valley and mountain top is the part that requires the most from us.

Throughout the journey of life, we are given the opportunity to embrace our purpose. Each day presents us a brand new opportunity to navigate through our struggles, to become more comfortable with who we are individually, and to change the standards that say who we have to be, what we have to do, and how we must get there. This is your moment to shine, don't pass this up! A special time of year for many is New Years. For most it's the time to spend with friends, enjoy delicious foods and drinks, shoot off fireworks plus a good ole time! However let me provoke your thought process for a second. When you hear New Year what comes to mind for you? I like to think of New Year as a new opportunity to be better at being YOU, new chances to make the right choices, and learn from the bad ones. We celebrate New Year as a welcome to new opportunities, and a farewell to the old. You and I have the chance to overcome, breakthrough and manifest the goals we have for the year. Something I once heard was promotion does not come from looking good, or showing up, It comes from putting in the work, time, and effort to reach your goal. I have spoken to a group of young adults on multiple occasions in different settings where the discussion topic and question was focused on, "Why does or doesn't God...?" God won't choose for us; he will warn you, instruct you, prompt you, guide you, encourage you to go the right direction, but at the end of the day, you are where you are because of the choices you made, the places you walked into, and the relationships you cultivated or even destroyed. Many people have a perception of God that he will choose for you, or allow you to, or even create an event that may make you question your faith and even God. It is common, but most of us allow our thoughts and emotions to dictate our choices. Where do you want to be this time next year? Are you living in TODAY, or choosing to stay in the THEN? Believe me, I have experience living in the THEN and not living in TODAY, and it affected me in such a way that I lost valuable time when I could have been working on being the best me NOW.

If you are someone who is currently reading this and is facing the constant detours, bumps, and fist shaking at the sky yelling, be reminded that the area of life most of us want to grow, cultivate, and embrace is our relationships. Let me ask you, what area in your relationships—your

relationship with God, in your family, or in your marriage
—is God calling you to grow or change?

Is God calling you to strengthen your relationship with him
or build better relationships with your family, pursue unity
in your workspace? When you begin to think about what
you want to see manifest in your life, some of you may be
thinking about investing more into your spouse and
developing a healthier marriage. Some of you may be
thinking about your job. Have you been in the same cubicle
for the past three years? No promotions but continued
expectations? How about your life in general? We wake up,
we have our morning routine, go to work or school, come
home and get ready to do it all over again. You and I both
hope to end up somewhere awesome, get promoted at our
job, cultivate a healthier relationship with God, family,
friends, even our spouse, but our destination will always be
decided by the path we choose with each turn and corner
we cut. Remember, the dash on a tombstone is just a line
that we see, but is the life you lived from your start to your
finish. We don't see the good choices, bad choices, the left
turns, and right turns on the dash, but what we see is a line
of legacy. Andy Stanley says it best, "Direction, not
intention, determines destination."

If there is anything I know about successful people, it's that
they don't say "I"; they say "we." This chapter focuses on

promoting our purpose, and embracing it. So just like there is a Father, Son, and Holy Spirit, this part of the chapter is part 3, which reveals the ultimate promotion. I call it "Elevated Sponsorship." Successful people aren't focused on how much they taught themselves, or how far they have come in their life; quite the opposite, to be frank. They give thanks and share their appreciation to all of those along the way that have pushed them to be the best, to never give up, and cheered them on even when they were at rock bottom.

Remember promotion is the activity that supports or provides active encouragement for the furtherance of a cause, venture, or aim. Throughout our life, we will reach limits and milestones. As you reach them, be reminded that the motion you are going in is forward. That right there is what promotion is. Moving in the steady forward direction. Knowing that each of us has encountered something, we have the ability to impact, encourage, and embrace, people. At the end of the day I truly believe it takes every single person to move in a forward motion to accomplish life. Successful people surround themselves with people that propel them forward. At the end of the day it's about the quality of friendships not quantity. Not everyone is going to choose to like you but that's Ok. There is a story in the Bible that I like to use when diving into this topic. The story of Naomi and Ruth is a very powerful story. Naomi was left with nothing after she had encountered a catastrophic famine and lost everything she had, including her husband and sons. Naomi tells Orpah and Ruth, her daughters-in-laws, to leave. With this command given, Orpah flees, and Ruth stays to support Naomi. She missed her husband and sons. At some point she felt she had no way to recover from this.

One thing was clear, though: Naomi was willing to step into a new season and continue to live her life to the fullest. With Ruth choosing to stay, Naomi didn't know what was in store for her.

Her life was about to manifest in accelerations, blessings, and elevation! She had thought she was empty, as would most of us if we lost everything, and those we loved. However, she had a realization that Ruth never left! Don't let who's missing block your vision from seeing who is by your side. Many of us shut down, lose focus, give up. It's the nature of being human: our thoughts and emotions hinder our sight of the light. Naomi began to invest into Ruth, listen to Ruth, coach Ruth and walk with Ruth. While Naomi was investing into Ruth's life, God began to orchestrate hope, purpose, and forgiveness in Naomi. Some of you are in a season of Naomi, and are in need of a Ruth. Well open your eyes. I am sure there are many Ruth's in your life right now; embrace them! The Book of Ruth is one of my favorites because it teaches us that we were not put on this earth for us, we were put on this earth to be a blessing and to be an impact on the next generation. This might be your season to promote, maybe your season to be called into a new season, a new chapter, a new way of living, growing, and dwelling in the community. It is not promised to be easy, and it will be uncomfortable at times. As we saw, Naomi lost everything, and her entire life took a 180. She realized that during this season of her life, she was given the opportunity to raise a young girl and empower her to be the best version she could be.

Through Ruth, God allowed Naomi to see her future, to help Ruth do what she couldn't do, but in order to get there, God instilled the wisdom and gifts into Naomi to be a mother, mentor, friend, and motivator to Ruth. Some of you are reading this book because you may be in a season in which you feel you have lost or been hurt, or maybe you are dealing with a situation that's been keeping you from growing. In order for you to get past your past, to grow from where you are now, you need to wake up to your present. Elevating people was something I woke up to. I was scared, afraid, angry, you name it. I didn't want to love people. I didn't want to live by the rules. But I had many Naomis love me, coach me, guide me, so that I could reach a season of my life to impact others. Don't miss out on your miracle because you are trying to be a Ruth when God wants you to be Naomi, and don't miss out on your miracle when you're trying to be Naomi when God wants you to be

Ruth. Just like the people in my life wanted me to win, I want the same thing for you! You never lose when you help others win!

Chapter 6 | Living the Prime Life

One of my most popular topical conversations I have with people is the focus on the Prime Life. Everyone always asks me what the Prime Life is. I'm almost positive that nobody wants to have a lame or boring life. Most of us also don't just want a pretty good life. It's safe to say that we all want an awesome life! We want our high school years to be the most fun. We want our summers to be epic and adventurous. We want to go through our college years and enjoy our opportunities while they last. And for some we want life after college to be full of adventure. We want our job to be something we love and that makes a difference. We want a spouse that rocks our world. We don't want mediocre. We don't want standard. We really don't even want pretty good. We each want the best quality, highest experience of life. We want the Prime Life. But when we look ahead at people who have already gone before us, some of the most successful people don't seem to be enjoying being in their prime. One of my favorite quarterbacks of all time, Peyton Manning, once said as he looked back on all of his achievements: "Man, is this it? I'm thinking there's got to be more than just this." When Manning won his Super Bowl, he knew that was when he would retire. He reached his prime in the NFL, and wanted that Super Bowl before he was done with his career. But how do we find the Prime Life? How do we get it? What's the secret formula? What if I told you that the reason so many people struggle to find it is because we're looking to the wrong source for making our lives all we want them to be. What if I told you that the things we think are going to give us "the life" aren't actually giving us "the life"? I was reading my Bible before I had done the podcast episode on the Prime Life, and I just think every time I read this scripture, Jesus made a great point. Here is what He said: **The thief comes only to steal and kill and destroy; I came that they may have life, and have it to the fullest. (John 10:10)** Sounds to me Jesus is saying that not only is the Prime Life possible, but that he came to make it happen for us. You see, the thief will come to take away your life and convince you that success is found in money, popularity, sex, stuff, pleasure, success, power, beauty, and a number of other things—Jesus says that a Prime Life is found in him! Too often the younger crowd is easily influenced by the social media, celebrities, and other sources that reroute us from that Prime Life. Nothing on the earth is eternal, so when we indulge the materialistic things we are susceptible to losing it too.

I used an example about credit cards when I was ministering to the young adults in Orlando. Imagine you apply for a credit card. You get approved. That company offers you a $500 credit limit with an APR of 24.99%.

Most of us if not all of us at one point didn't really think too much about the APR. We cared more about the limit we received. I remember when I got my first credit card and I felt like a champion. Like, man, I got $1,000 in my hand and I can spend it on things.

Well, not really knowing how APR worked at the time, I ended up using my card, making payments monthly, but establishing interest at the same time. In life, the devil plays as the credit card company. He will make you think you have it all, but will charge interest on your life because you are using "his service."

The point is that the enemy will taint what he is doing to look good, and we fall into the "Oh man, I got a $1,000 limit," or "Look, I have this house, car, boat…" You see, God wants us all to be wealthy, and fruitful, but be reminded the enemy will manipulate the Prime Life making it seem it's the stuff we have, or the car we drive. So that's what this verse is saying. That living in your prime really depends on whose hands your life is in. When your life is in his hands, he will wield your life, use it, lead it, play it to the fullest. **Your best life is found only by placing it in the best hands. The Prime Life starts with Jesus.**

ABILITY VS. AVAILABILITY

Have you ever had a "Who, me?" moment? A moment when you thought you weren't qualified for something—like an assignment, a role in a play, a step up in leadership at your job, maybe even a position in your school's student government…but then you get tapped on the shoulder and you find yourself thinking, "Who, me?" Many of us have that moment and even when we least expect it. Recently I did some research and found a survey sponsored by the National Board of Education. They had asked students if they saw themselves excelling at something in middle school or high school, and over 80 percent said no. It is unfortunate that such a larger percentage of students didn't feel they had what it takes to excel or to succeed. So when Jesus says that you can have "life to the full," many people don't have a problem believing this is possible…they're just skeptical that it's possible for them! If you recall a unique character in the Bible, Joshua, he had an encounter in which Joshua felt God tapping him on the shoulder. God says to Joshua, **"Moses, my servant is dead." (Joshua 1:2)**. That's a huge deal. Joshua had HUGE shoes to fill. We know that Moses was the warrior prophet of Israel who rained down plagues on the superpower Egypt and led an entire nation out of slavery. That is the guy Joshua is supposed to replace?! This put Joshua in a position he hadn't been in before. And he evidently did what most of us do in the face of big opportunity and God's big plans for our lives: he became acutely aware of how unqualified he was. He became acutely aware of who he was NOT, constantly asking himself, "Who, me? I'm NOT Moses. I'm NOT a great leader."

I'm NOT a mighty warrior. I'm NOT even that spiritual. Does this sound familiar? Of course it does! All of us at some point feel unqualified. However, if we focus on who we are NOT, it will get in the way of who God sees us becoming. If we are not careful, who we are NOT is going to get in the way of what God wants to do in our life. If we are not careful, who we are NOT is going to keep us from ever experiencing the Prime Life that God has in mind for us. So I love this part of the Bible because God gives Joshua a pep talk:

As I was with Moses, so I will be with you; I will never leave you nor forsake you. Be strong and courageous, because you will lead these people to inherit the land I swore to their ancestors to give them. Be strong and very courageous. Be careful to obey all the law my servant Moses gave you; do not turn from it to the right or to the left, that you may be successful wherever you go. Keep this Book of the Law always on your lips; meditate on it day and night, so that you may be careful to do everything written in it. Then you will be prosperous and successful. Have I not commanded you?

Be strong and courageous. Do not be afraid; do not be discouraged, for the Lord your God will be with you wherever you go. (Joshua 1:6-9)

You may have read this a few times. Did you notice God repeating anything to Joshua? Anything in particular? He kept mentioning to be strong and courageous. He would remind him to go where He told him, do what He told him, and not back down no matter how scary it gets or impossible it seems. God knows where we are going, and when He gives the instructions to Joshua, God also gives them to us. God makes it clear that he is not concerned with us being ABLE to pull off everything that he has planned— he is concerned about us being willing to say yes. **God is not concerned with our ABILITY but with our AVAILABILITY.**

The first step of experiencing the Prime Life is getting over who you are not and simply making yourself available to the God who is. He's ready. Are you?

CHANGING YOUR CIRCUMSTANCES
Sometimes it can feel like your life is anything but prime. In fact, it often feels the opposite. That's because many of us feel like our life is ordinary, dysfunctional, or tragic. We feel like our life is either ordinary and nothing unique, maybe it feels as if its falling apart and dysfunctional, or it

may even feel tragic because of an unforeseen event that may have occurred. So what do you do with this? If we want to live the Prime Life, what do we do when our circumstances are ordinary, dysfunctional, or tragic? What do we do when we feel like this is what is standing between you and the life God wants for you? Well, God doesn't promise to change your circumstance. Take the story of Joseph, for example. First, his brothers sold him into slavery, and then he was set up by Potiphar's wife and thrown into prison for a crime he didn't commit.

And yet, he winds up being put in charge of the prison because the Lord was with him! And it was from here that God was setting the stage for what was to come. Eventually God would connect Joseph with the Pharaoh's cupbearer. He would enable Joseph to correctly interpret a dream for him. This in turn made its way to Pharaoh who some time later had a dream that he needed interpreting. So God gave Joseph an audience with Pharaoh himself straight from prison. God is with Joseph again to interpret Pharaoh's dream, and Pharaoh is so moved by how God is with Joseph that he makes a crazy decision:

So Pharaoh said to Joseph, "I hereby put you in charge of the whole land of Egypt." Then Pharaoh took his signet ring from his finger and put it on Joseph's finger. He dressed him in robes of fine linen and put a gold

chain around his neck. 43 He had him ride in a chariot as his second-in-command, and people shouted before him, "Make way!" (Genesis 41:41-42)

Joseph becomes second in command of the most powerful nation on earth. You want to talk about the Prime Life. Oh man, this guy lived it. You better believe that when Joseph looked back on his life he didn't think it was small or ordinary. No way. It was more than he ever dreamed of. And here's the deal: that would never have happened if God simply changed his circumstances when Joseph wanted him to.

That's why God did something better: he used them. And that's what you need to know: **often God doesn't want to change our circumstances; he wants to use them.** Your circumstances aren't an annoyance or an inconvenience to God; no, they're probably the very thing he's going to use, against all odds and against all expectations, to lead you where he wants you to be.

So your job, and a huge next step in pursuing the Prime Life, is to change your approach to your current circumstances. Here are three ways you can do that:
1. See them through God's eyes. Close your eyes on ordinary, dysfunctional, and tragic, and open them with the lens of "What could God do here?!?" What does God see

here? If he took Joseph from prison to the Prime Life, what does he want to do with this?

2. Make a plan for them. Make a plan for how you are going to take over the world from where you are right now. Don't wait for some lottery ticket to come along. That's not how God works most of the time. Most of the time his plan is not to change your circumstances, but use them. So we have to be ready. We have to start tuning in. How is God going to take something meant for evil and use it for something beautiful and big?

3. Do the best you can with what you have. Change the way you see your circumstances. Make a plan for them. And then just do the best you can with what you have. Do the best you can, just like Joseph, and trust God to bless it.

FINDING YOUR LIFE

Being a follower of Jesus can be hard—especially when you are in school. People make fun of you, they laugh behind your back, or you can't attend events because you're at church. Following Jesus can be unpleasant and at times even unpopular, and you've probably asked yourself the question: **is it worth it?** This is the question that lies right at the heart of the Prime Life.

This question more than any other is one that's at the epicenter of your chance to live life to the fullest. This question has the potential to change your life. And there was a time when Jesus spoke directly about this question.

Then Jesus said to His disciples, "If anyone wishes to come after Me, he must deny himself, and take up his cross and follow Me." (Matthew 16:24)

Jesus decides to keep it real and says, "Listen, if you follow me, I mean all in follow me, it will absolutely cost you something." He's not sugar-coating it. His honesty makes you wonder if you should even bother following him fully —but Jesus speaks to this question too: "For whoever wishes to save his life will lose it; but whoever loses his life for My sake will find it." (Matthew 16:25) What Jesus is saying here is that if you want to get the life He wants for you—the Prime Life— you'll have to let go of the life you have. But if you do that, God promises that you will have the most amazing, significant, full, awesome, adventurous, crazy good life that you could ever live. And second, He promises that this life will be eternal. Jesus died and rose from the dead not just to give us life for a couple of decades but life that goes on forever. That's the kind of life we're talking about here. That's why it's worth it to follow Jesus—or start following Jesus—even when you know sometimes it's going to be unpleasant and unpopular.

Because those who wish to save their lives will lose it. But those who lose their life, they are the ones who find it. And in light of that, it's a no-brainer. But you have to decide.

Chapter 7 | Innovation Sparks Life

Throughout the past few years, I have learned ways to be more innovative. The key to being able to innovate is that one should be able to think outside the box. Innovation sparks new beginnings and opportunities for us to live out the best in life, and when we become familiar with it, it serves its purpose for us. Innovation is made up of significant components and each is vital to the next. Part of becoming a better person and better Christian is being able to create, collaborate, facing your obstacles and seeing the opportunity within them, and finally learning that failure is part of life.

If we dive into the first chapter of the Bible, we would read a famous story, in which God creates mankind in his image. At this point, we know very little about who God really is —we don't yet know about His love, His power, or His justice. Pretty much all we know about God at this point is that He is the creator. What this means is that, regardless of whether you feel creative or not, and regardless of how people perceive your creativity, we are all designed in the image of a creator, so we are all creative people. Often I will spark a conversation with people and they usually say to me that they don't consider themselves to be creative. I beg to differ. My reply to people often sounds like this: "Well, if you want to be more creative, the best way to be more creative, or even recognize your creativeness is to spend more time with the creator." When I am in the presence of the creator, He fuels my creativity. For example, this book. Over the past few years I was on and off with this book. I would write three chapters, edit, and then take a break. It wasn't that I neglected the presence of God, I just needed to be completely soaked in His presence to focus, and write. The writer and pastor Erwin McManus writes: "To create is to reflect the image of God. To create is an act of worship." One of the easiest traps to fall into when it comes to the topic of innovation is boxing what innovation looks like into a specific definition or category. I have seen this with myself, and even others. It is easy to limit yourself when you try to recreate innovation. Innovation is not recreating, it is finding a way to do things in a better, more appealing way.

I don't know about you, but when people start talking about innovation I often think of people coming up with new ideas, collaborating in small groups, and developing ideas to bring to the table. Because we are human, we are tempted to box innovation into a particular look or style, because we have this stereotype of what modern creativity looks like.

The great entrepreneur Henry Ford once said, "Coming together is a beginning, staying together is a process, and working together is success." Mr. Ford utilized collaboration to design and manufacture the first cars that people could afford, and in turn innovated a whole industry. One of the major keys to be great at innovating, is understanding that collaboration is a foundational aspect to elevating and growing. The Websters Dictionary defines "collaboration" as "the action of working with someone to produce something; two things that were separate are now together." Look around you. In the world in which we live, the fruits of collaboration are clear to us. We collaborate because we don't want to limit our wisdom, or even the creativeness of others. Several years ago I started collaborating with Adler, who launched his 24hrsinaday organization that innovates health and wellness to focus on bettering physical, spiritual, and mental health. When the 24hrsinaday franchise broke ground in the US for the first time, people had been connecting and wanting to be part of the growing organization. I met with Adler on multiple occasions to collaborate on the growth and success of his fitness program franchise. Innovation can only come through collaboration. Many of you have worn shoes or maybe clothing from the major sports brand Adidas, which was founded in 1949 by a German gentleman named Adi Dassler. The result of collaboration, time, and efforts to innovative a product line resulted in one of the major brands worn worldwide. But ultimately, God himself demonstrated the power of collaboration when he gave us some key life instructions in Matthew 28:18: "Therefore go and make disciples of all nations, baptizing them in the name of the Father and of the Son and of the Holy spirit." What I take from this is that the great commission requires great collaboration. We face our greatest challenge all the time and that is collaborating with Christ. Of course, you can collaborate with people and build a brand, or you can collaborate with Jesus and build the church. God is a collaborating God and he made us in his image, so when we collaborate we reflect the characteristics of God. As you think about the possibilities to collaborate in your sphere, be mindful of the importance of the right motivation.

Let's take a change of direction and focus on the Book of Exodus, where we read about a great hero of the faith, Moses, who was asked by God to gather his people and lead them out of Egypt, the place where they were enslaved. For Moses, he had to take serious risk that came with numerous obstacles: the uprooting of families, Pharaoh's refusal to let them go, and the rebellion of some of his people.

Moses began to take the people out of Israel, and they ended up at the Red Sea. The sea was in front of them and the Egyptians were behind them, and it seemed like there was no hope left, as they were surrounded with no way out. Of course, we all know the miraculous story of Moses leading the people through the Red Sea, but what we often forget is that Moses's obstacle was actually his greatest opportunity for success. It was because of the Red Sea that the Egyptians were defeated, and God led the Israelites to safety. Our obstacles are a part of our life, and they will always seem to throw themselves at you when you try to take on an opportunity to innovate. For you and me, obstacles are going to look different, but if innovation is a Godly trait, and we are using it for His glory, we can trust that our obstacles are actually opportunities in disguise. One of my favorite Bible stories is David and Goliath. If you recall, David was tasked with fighting a giant much bigger than himself, and rather than listening to the conventional wisdom of the time (which was that of wearing armor and fighting Goliath like a warrior), David took a stick and a rubber band, latched a few stones in his gizmo, and defeated Goliath in a way that had never been done before. Both Moses and David were faced with numerous roadblocks, yet they both knew God called them to something, so each man in his own circumstance placed trust in God. Every day we get a chance to innovate. Embrace your innovativeness!

Most people I have spoken with will see where they need to innovate, yet each of us comes to a crossroad where we find it difficult to implement this change. I believe the number one reason why we don't act on implementing innovative solutions is the fear of failure. I know this because I have done it myself—when I first really started working on a platform that would be used to impact many, I wanted it to change the way people would learn, grow, and connect at a new level. I had seen a new way of doing things when I launched a platform to make it easier for people navigate an online Christ-centered hub.

Over the years I knew it would be better in the long run, but I didn't pursue it, because the thought of failing overshadowed the thought of succeeding. Diving in to Isaiah 43:18 it says, "Do not remember the former things, or ponder the things of the past." What this basically is highlighting is that thinking back to times of failure to invalidate taking action in the present is unhealthy. Fear of failure often will prevent us from pursuing innovation, and it stops us from trying things and taking risks. Your failures should not cause you to run away from God; they should cause you to run towards him! As a leader, I have started thinking about how I can build a culture where it is OK to take a risk and where it is OK to fail, a culture where our failings do not define us as a failure. It makes it easier to connect with others on levels that most wouldn't imagine. I have learned over the years that people aren't looking for a social gathering, rather a family, and knowing if you fail, God will use those opportunities to build you.

I want to continue on talking about innovation and how we live in a society in a world where we are constantly looking for more effective ways to innovate. This is a very important aspect because I feel like a lot of people asked me this question and it's about how social media is really a platform for innovation. I look back on the people that I have encountered and I'll talk to you and I realize that so many of us utilize social media as a platform to engage with followers to help them grow, change, and navigate through life. You and I both, as I've mentioned before, have a creative aspect of ourselves. Now understand that when you were innovative you were learning to become more effective, becoming more rational, becoming more authentic and organic in your own form of living. "This Is Me" was developed on a simple yet powerful idea and no matter what background you have, you have a mindset to innovate a way to expose yourself to a form of creativity. Many of us fear failure. We have opportunities versus obstacles, and we focus so much on what we can't do when we have so much that we can do.

The average American spends two hours on social media a day. Whether it's scrolling through the feed, liking someone's recent photo, there is a significant amount time spent on the social media platforms we enjoy. This simply means that we spend more time focusing on what people are complaining about, what people want to be angry about, because we utilize social media as a dumping ground for our unintended emotions. Social media can be used to elevate the growth of yourself and others. Many of you have probably seen that I was on Facebook, that I am on Instagram, and I utilize my social media platforms as a place to elevate people on a global level. You may have seen some of the quotes I've posted on social media simply referring to daily reminders for you to be the best version of you. I try to approach different aspects of life with a mindset that there's good and there's potential for optimism in every situation.

I would like to point out that each of us has the potential to innovate. Most people when they hear innovation or to innovate, I would imagine they think of an invention, new idea, or maybe the evolution of a product. I want you to think about your life and ask yourself how am I innovating my life? How am I taking the steps to maximize my growth? I personally believe we cut ourselves short of our innovative abilities. I can understand that not everyone would call themselves the most creative, but this is the misconception about innovation. Being innovative is being able to produce and new idea, or concept. Think about the prime life as the new idea. The ability to advance in life is within in reach.

I encourage you to find time to write down the new steps you are taking to live a more prime life. These steps don't have to be complicated. They can be simple. Writing them down gives us a subconscious accountability that streamlines as a way to remind ourselves to become disciplined of the innovations of our life. For me an innovation would include the ability to communicate with people. For a long time I struggled communicating with people. I was afraid often times than not. Sometimes it takes time to develop the confidence to operate within the innovations we establish for our life. Needless to say, the innovations are always going to come back to point to God. I recall I had posted something on my Instagram page about having a kingdom mindset and doing everything for the kingdom of God. If you jump into the Book of Matthew chapter 6, you'll see it is talking about not being stressed and not being worried, trusting God and doing everything for him. This is only the beginning and the best is yet to come. Let your innovation be your navigation and let the creation be your identification because God is giving you a gift, multiple gifts, to excel and to elevate. Go for it. Next time you feel like you're not where you want to be or maybe you feel like you're not creative enough, remember three things. First, remember the first story in the Bible where God created the earth. He created each and every one of us in his own creation, nothing better, nothing more powerful than knowing we are created by the Almighty

Creator, the best innovator. The second thing to remember is to always remember innovation is the new ideas or methods we learn to dominate our journey with the best approach possible. Find opportunities to overcome obstacles in your life. What are you waiting for? The third and final point I would like for you to take in is that innovation gives us identification. It's who we are. Think of it like this. A wise man once told me a brilliant analogy. Imagine humanity as a puzzle. Each piece in the box is different. Say this puzzle consists of 5000 pieces, that's 5000 unique pieces that are needed to complete the puzzle. We all can't be the same size, shape, or attach to the other pieces perfectly, however each piece is needed to complete the puzzle. At the end of the day, Innovation gives each of us a unique approach to life. No person will do the same thing as another the same way. Don't ever limit yourself to reach your potential because it is easy to do so.

Chapter 8 | The Vulnerable Journey

I am victorious. One of the greatest things about writing is that you get the opportunity to revisit places in your life. Writing is a platform for an author to dig a bit deeper into their life while focusing on channeling their thoughts and feelings with their readers. I can't stress this enough, I want each of you to know that I believe you have potential, and that every step of the way is reachable if you believe. One of the greatest parts of my journey so far has been learning to be more vulnerable. Most people would describe vulnerability as a sign of uncertainty, risky, a degree of emotional exposure that can make us feel unstable or lose control. My personal viewpoint of vulnerability is the opportunity to find personal healing and forgiveness when stepping out of our own comfort zone. It took me several years before I truly could embody the opportunity to forgive myself and finally forgive others. I experienced a lot of guilt and shame, which led me to a crossroad to find healing. Over the past few years, I have had the humbling opportunities to speak with different people about their walk in life. In every conversation, there was always this raw and authentic atmosphere. As if there were no boundaries for emotions, thoughts, and conversation. A place where two people could truly and freely speak from within. It's not common to dig beneath the superficial elements of man, but when it is done, there is a sense of healing and faith that can arise.

After listening to the stories of each individual over time, It gave me perspective on how related we are as humans. Each of us is broken, and finding that inner strength to share such personal material, that is breathtaking. At times in our life we face moments where there is silence or no movement. We begin to question our well-being, our personal growth, and maybe even our steps. The inner self becomes overwhelmed, and becomes unsure or uneasy with the path that we are taking. We should take a moment to realize that the only time we should ever look back is to see how far we have come. The goals we reach, the traumas we have overcome, the relationships we built, or let go, this is growth. We must be honest with ourselves FIRST. We don't change or grow for others, we change and grow for ourselves.

I spent most of my childhood and teenage years seeking other's affirmation because I believed my opinion of myself was not worthy. I was always looking for ways to fit in, instead of focusing on just being me. I will say this is definitely easier said than done. Now most of us experience this throughout stages of becoming an adult because we are aware of judgment, opinion, and status. I'm no different to anyone who reads my book. As a matter of fact, I am broken. I am not perfect. Therefore, I believe we have to become more aware of our personal experiences because those moments are teaching moments.

Some readers are looking for motivation, but others of you might be going through a more significant season. A word that comes to mind when I become overwhelmed, or in need of redirection is "redirection." Kind of like with a GPS. Sometimes we miss an exit. It's easy to become upset at the situation. However, have you ever noticed that your GPS reroutes you? Not once did she yell at you for missing the turn, she simply rerouted you. This is an example of redirecting. The GPS executes the next best way to reach the end point as seamlessly as possible. There are times when in life we miss the exit, but we are rerouted. It takes discipline to seamlessly reroute when we miss our exits. We continue to execute our goals, dreams, and growth by continuing, not stopping. The destination inputted on the GPS never changed, just your journey. Your destination in life also never changes. What happens between point A and point B, that's up to you. When I first sat down, and wrote down a few bullet points to get this book going, I saw the finish line. I knew that one day I could say I published a book. Over the years I took breaks because I was discouraged on my path. There were times I would get writer's block. Even at times I was challenged by others on the thought that writing a book in my twenties was ridiculous. Detours can be the difference in how your journey is seen. Each of us has control over the way we see the detour.

Along the way of developing my book, I asked myself many times how much I want to share with people. Of course we all have parts of our life we feel comfortable talking about, which is normal. But the parts that I am talking about are parts that bring out core emotions and can touch someone who may be going through a season in life. I used to think that my story was one I'd put on a shelf and never talk about. But being able to see how others are going through something, that's where you become transparent. This became a focal point for me. I want to be as transparent as I possibly can with you. Every day I find that I connect with people and, in sharing, learn where they are in life. I may not be going through exactly what you are, but at the most we all have those struggles and broken pieces that we hold on to. We are professionals at tucking away our fears, traumas, experiences into a shoe box, taping it shut and putting it on the bookshelf for us to never touch again. I get it. I spent a large part of my life hiding and tucking away. For most, we do our best to not think about the past events that hurt us, saddened us, or even altered us. It can be hard to revisit and let go. Vulnerability is fundamental to our development as humans. It has never been about winning or losing for me.

It has been about having faith and fortitude to show up and be seen when the outcome is unknown. It can be very tough to do that if we are always in a state of fear of what others may think or see of us. Perhaps you have associated it with weakness, hurt, or betrayal. These are the deep-rooted emotions that you and I experience when we open up to people. It is perfectly OK to have experiences that have shifted your emotional well-being. Our association with vulnerability depends on our focus and awareness. There isn't a single human I've come across in my life that doesn't experience pain. I think most can agree that vulnerability is often associated with pain or fear. For each of us, we handle and overcome pain differently. However, there is a key point that is worth sharing with you. Healing is a process and each of us reaches it at a different pace. I used to think healing was a one size fits all, but this is not the case. Healing from my personal pain was overwhelming, but learning to undertake a process of self-evaluation gave me hope. Becoming aware of your inner self and understanding who you are on a deeper level is so important. Become more interested and curious about why you react to something when your "sensors" have been manipulated. Become a student of vulnerability, and watch how it gives us the opportunity to shine light on the broken parts of who we are, which then simplifies the algorithm of self-renewal. I invite you to sit down with yourself and write down those past events you ignore or dwell on. Ask yourself what is it that you want as an outcome from the situation. Be selfish and intentional about becoming curious and digging deeper into who you are. I didn't really know how to do this at first, but being honest with myself and forgiving myself, made it easier to be more intentional about your self awareness. Being aware that there is trauma, hurt, pain, betrayal in your life isn't a bad thing. As a matter of fact this is only the first step for healing. I used to hold back from change. I shut down, and would have rather find a way to ovoid change. For the longest time, I was afraid to share parts of my life. I didn't want people to know that I had an attachment issue, or share that I was intentional about making my parents suffer emotionally, and mentally. I was verbally, emotionally and physically abusive towards my mother. Most children who are adopted behave this way as an "escape mechanism" due to the detachment developed in early childhood. I later on did more research and found that this behavior stems from the initial biological relationship between the infant and mother. If there is no secure attachment between the biological mother and child, this can lead to the trust barrier of the person(s) who adopt the child. This then leads to behaviors such as anxiety, anger, sadness, and abuse towards others especially the mother who is the primary nurturer. While it came from a place of fear, anger, and sadness, my mother never deserved it. A few years after giving my life to Christ, I asked my parents both for forgiveness for I knew the Bible says to honor your mother and father so that your days are longer on the earth. As I may have mentioned before, healing is not a one side fits all, however to this day my relationship with my mother is impeccable. I love my parents, and it is important to note that my parents NEVER gave up, and that was vital. I encourage parents who adopt to never give up on their child. As I have gotten older, I spent extensive time doing research on the behavior of children who are adopted and those that are not adopted however have experienced traumatic events in their life. Much of the behaviors come from early detachment and early brain development affected by trauma, neglect and other circumstances. I was hurting, and my only way to communicate this was to hurt others. I wanted my parents to feel my fear, to feel how angry and sad I was.

Understanding the root cause for our hurt can benefit us. I share a common root to many young adults and children I have spoken with. I recall speaking to some younger adults who have been adopted from other parts of the world. One of them shared his experience in the orphanage in El Salvador when he was a young boy. He shared that he would eat from the garbage cans, run around with no supervision, and the list continues. Shortly I began to see a pattern in the kids' stories. Another shared her story where she had to grow up fairly quickly and take care of her other two sisters. Their mother made poor choices, which hindered her from being able to take care of her own children. While those stories were shared by people who were adopted, I also have had some powerful conversations with people who weren't adopted. Growing up being verbally abused by their mother, and running away from home because there was a sense of comfort and safety when fleeing from the danger. Dealing with parents who divorce, or losing a parent to a tragic event. I could go on and on with the list, but the point I am making is that adopted or not we all are broken, have pieces scattered, and we don't always have the strength to put them together. Vulnerability is an act of courage and doesn't happen overnight. When we can commit to merge with our inner self at an authentic level, instead of hiding behind a facade to appease others, healing begins. For the one who has been rejected, abused, raped, disowned, bullied, lost, or experienced struggle, I want my words to wrap you and hug you. I want you to know how much worth you have. You have the strength to be YOU, and share your story to impact those that need to know it will be okay. It is never guaranteed to be easy or an overnighter, but start right now by igniting the flame to generate love, courage, and change in those you encounter. I encourage you to lift your chin, and feel my love and understanding through my words. I like this quote by Haruki Murakami: "What happens when people open their hearts? They get better." Often we retaliate, which then leads to suffering. I often found myself looking for the outlet that only temporarily solved the issue. I would become defensive and would throw up walls to keep myself from having to respond to the situation. The unfortunate thing that most of us associate with vulnerability is the disconnect with others. We convince ourselves that the people we encounter won't understand, or they may judge us. I invite you to try taking a different approach. Instead of thinking what others may say, remember that they are also broken and may have not found the strength to overcome. Going a little further, have you ever asked yourself if you understand your circumstance? If you are judging yourself? While we are quick to hide from others and what they may see or think, have you considered that maybe you are hiding from yourself? Believe me, I am the first to admit that I have replayed this over and over again. It took me several years to become aware that the thoughts and emotions associated with my fear of what others may see or think of me started with me.

Vulnerability, as we know, is fundamental. Self-awareness is as well. I believe that self-awareness is one of the most challenging attributes as a human. We were designed with biases and emotional patterns that would prevent us from being self-aware. The importance of being self-aware doesn't lie strictly in knowing what is currently taking place, but in being able to focus on what we are thinking, doing, and feeling. However, not just in the present, but also in the past and future. We develop habits and routine based off what we think, do, and feel.

How many of you would say you are living a perfect life? How about a normal life? What defines these, though? If I can be honest, none of us can answer either question because perfection doesn't exist here on earth. And normal? Nobody is living a normal life. A normal or perfect life isn't realistic. We like to think our lives are that way, but nobody on this earth goes from birth to death without experiences, and that's just that. If we are honest with ourselves, more times than not when we face a moment that challenges us, or shifts us into an uncomfortable position, we tend to go into reaction mode. If I had to describe this reactive mindset, I would say that people will take that moment, toss it in a box, and throw it away hoping that it would never show up again. We try to block them out, ignore them, and can we truthfully do that? Maybe temporarily, but if we don't, we face the circumstances they can lead to: negative thoughts, possible anxiety or depression. Instead of hiding, wouldn't it make more sense to let it go? Let's just say someone you work with or live with is doing something that is bothering you. Think about your response to this person. Most of us will speak up and say something to that person. You have that conversation and most of the time there is a mutual respect and the issue is resolved. You feel better about getting it off your chest, right? Well, what is different about the circumstances in life? A lot, I know. It requires a new level of emotions and courage.

Perhaps we can apply the mindset that healing comes from within. One must be self-aware, enable yourself to be honest with yourself and then learn to embrace the circumstances that you have been through. I know this seems far off topic; however, each moment is a contributing factor to your walk on this earth. When I was sixteen years old, I became aware of this concept. I used to wish my childhood years were better, or that they never happened. I used to think to myself, What if it were different? What If I didn't cause so much hurt and pain to others? What if I cared about my grades? I gradually learned that every single encounter is a building block. I'm not saying everything was right, but those moments happened, I learned from them, and now I'm taking those lessons learned to teach people that once you come to realize that everything happens for a reason, then you begin to make the changes in your life. Being vulnerable and having self-awareness can reach many areas in our life. Our goals, dreams, taking the strides of risk to get to the next part of your life. We become comfortable and when this happens, we can easily neglect areas of our life. How many of us stop to think about where we are going? How many times have you set a goal and you might have forgotten about the journey? Most of us strive to reach goals and destinations in life. However, as important as the destination is, it is also vital to embrace the journey as well. Throughout this book I made sure to make connections with you because I realized the importance of the journey. We each have our own approach to life, but for the most part we strive to reach the end. It's not just about starting and finishing, but the more steps you took to get there, the experiences you gain along the way, the better you understand why you had to go that distance to reach your destination. In this chapter I wanted to dive a bit deeper into the idea of completely embracing being vulnerable. It is never easy to share, and some of us aren't comfortable sharing, which is OK. Coming from my own personal walk in life, I have become more familiar with my journey and observing that as long as you keep your destination in mind and focus on the moment, you will eventually reach the places you want to reach. Most of us have education, careers, relationships, financials in mind for our destination. I love it. Embrace it, and focus on the steps you take to reach these goals. When I started writing this book, I had no idea how I was going to even start. For one, writing has never been something I considered to be a strength. It's funny how in life sometimes we take extra steps and find out a new thing or two about ourselves. Personally, that's what makes this whole journey so fun. Could you imagine if life was already solved, and there was no motivation or purpose to go out and venture this thing called life? Like I've expressed before, connecting with people, learning about them, embracing who they are is what I live for. As I get older I understand why I am here. I hope that by the end of the book, the word "elevation" isn't just said in reference to mountains, but to actual life. The strides you make, the journey you're on, the mountaintops you reach, that's what it's all about.

In my most recent years, I have made it my own personal habit to say hello to people everywhere I go. Creating that personal connection with someone has more value than money. Most of us own an iPhone or Android device, which we use to post on our social media pages, browse the latest news, hold interesting conversations, and complete day-to-day tasks. The sad reality though is that we spend too much time looking down at these screens. It takes time away from our day-to-day interactions with people we live with, work with, and even could run into on our way to the local coffee shop! The point I'm trying to make is that we often neglect our journey. The now. We often don't even realize that we are neglecting the journey. On multiple occasions I've attended young adult connect nights within the community hosted by different groups, and spent time talking and learning from other young adults as they venture through life. Interesting enough, listening to some of the young adults speak, they support the unpopular opinion of embracing the journey as well as the destination. They care about failure and struggle and how important it is. It always makes me happy to be invited and share my approach of the unpopular opinion. A great number of us are solely destination-minded, therefore we focus on the end and less so on why or where we are going. The living in the moment mindset is a false perception of "embracing the journey." As mentioned earlier in the book, when you climb your mountain, you start at a starting point, most likely the bottom of the mountain. As you make your way up, you are experiencing the elevation change, the scenery, and so on. However, you have your destination already figured out prior to the journey as this is simply a subconscious thought or landmark we create for the sole purpose of success and human satisfaction.

For me, this book can be the "Start - Journey- Destination" example. I needed a focus point to write on. Since I typed the first paragraph of this book, I added, I deleted, contemplated, and every so often took a little writer's break due to writer's block. Quite frankly, I find it interesting that people want to set their mind on the destinations, and we forget about what we're doing and why we're doing it. Sometimes I think that as people we acknowledge that there is going to be a struggle with knowledge, that there's going to be some part of life that we have to expand on, that we're going to have to experience things that are a little more difficult at times. But then at the same time I think that we also find ourselves integrating the point A, point B mindset. How many of you have used a GPS that has gotten you from point A to point B? Many years ago I remember speaking to a younger group of adults about the GPS, which is also known as a global positioning system. I took a little twist on it and called it the God's Positioning System. So if you think about Point A as your starting point of your life, maybe right now you're at A, and you're really eager to get to point B. However, in order for us to get to point B, we have to experience the journey. The reason that I go into depth about the journey and how this is related to the elevation of each individual is that each day we're focused on growing, we focus on becoming better at being ourselves and therefore we have to understand that a part of growing and part of change, a part of acknowledging the elevation of our own individual life, requires us to go down this journey. I think that sometimes we find ourselves wanting to reroute or change direction because we feel like we can't accomplish certain tasks that are at hand. However, sometimes you have to look at it and say, "Well, this is why I'm here and this is what I'm doing." So I wanted to kind of imagine this GPS mindset: I'm here at point A, I'm trying to get to point B. Have you ever traveled on a major interstate or a road with maybe an accident or some kind of construction going on, and all the sudden your GPS will reroute you? How many of you have gotten frustrated because now you need an additional thirty minutes to your drive? I know I've been there, I know we've all experienced some sort of detour that had created tension or frustration in our life. So how do you overcome or how do you acknowledge that the journey is an important aspect of your life? You don't just go from A to B. No one can teleport, but recognize that the struggle is going to be an aspect of your growth. When I started writing this book I was focused on acknowledging my life, acknowledging it from my perspective on how I had to go through certain experiences that have ultimately bettered me as a person. Yes, there are going to be times where you will be detoured, but one thing that I want you to acknowledge right here is, what if Siri rerouted you because you missed an exit when you weren't paying attention?

Sometimes I think that we get to a point in our life and we are not really paying attention. We miss what we're supposed to turn off on and we wonder why. I guess sometimes in life we miss exits, sometimes we get rerouted, sometimes we just find or selfs going the extra mile because sometimes you need to do that. With all those beans, all this being said, I realize that sometimes when you find yourself in a place where you feel like you have to struggle or maybe you're encountering these moments in life that really are shaping you to be better at being who you are, that is a part of the whole excursion of life. However, one of the major things that I share with people is that elevating as an individual requires you to acknowledge the success, the failures, the struggles, the moments that you're going to feel overwhelmed. You have to pass the breaking point of comfort. This is an additional point that I want to talk about in this chapter: the breaking point of comfort. You have no limit; the only limit that you give is the one that you give to yourself. Too many times I feel like we make excuses, we blame people, we blame our circumstances on why we can't do something or why we do not have these things in our lives. The faster that we realize and the more optimistic we are, utilizing our time wisely and managing our goals the way were supposed to, we realize that growth doesn't happen overnight.

In the last three years or so, I have had the opportunity to learn many incredible life lessons. Of those many, there are a few I live by. While I was attending Basic Military Training, Master Sergeant Brooks taught us to be comfortable uncomfortable. At first it didn't make much sense, but it did once he explained to us what he meant. Being comfortable or being content is easy; however, when you move, when you strive, when you struggle, you will find that you will have more uncomfortable moments that help you build resilience in your daily life. Most times I found myself reevaluating how can I do this, how can I do this better, how can I strive to be more successful. I have come across some very creative people in my life. People are constantly creating more effective ways to be better; it's just part of how we are. Recall the chapters about mountains and valleys. It's like sometimes we have to take a few steps back in order move a few steps forward. I believe I've used the GPS example a bit, but here is another approach using the example. In this case we utilize the GPS to navigate a path we input, and it ultimately gets us to our destination. Now imagine you are going on a road trip to Washington State, but you do not use a GPS to get there. For some odd reason it won't work. How would you respond? Where would you begin? What can we do to find the solution? In theory, this would also go with the God's Positioning System as well. Ideally, we need God to get to our final, and without him, we really can't navigate through life truly trusting the course of direction is or isn't correct. If you have been lost before, you may be panicked, worried, or even frustrated. However, this is common, but not most tactical. Now let's change the scenario for a bit: your GPS does work, and you use it to get to Washington State. I can guarantee that you and I will feel much more confident and secure with reaching our destination. Why? Because you inputted two constant points, while the course of action along the way may change. Sometimes being comfortable can be good, depending on the situation. With

God being our captain of life, I would be comfortable with his guidance, while he may ask, direct, or show where you need to go, trust his guidance.

The breaking point of comfort will change you and how you may respond to life. The moment that you face an uncomfortable situation, it is a default response to revert to a state of comfort. While it is nice to be comfortable, growth and change happens in your uncomfortable moments. There is an equilibrium between the comfort of life in the discomfort of life. Many of us are afraid of being uncomfortable, and that is normal. However, being in this uncomfortable state it gives us the opportunity to build resilience and strength. With the peaks of life, there are also valleys. Sometimes you are going to have the opportunity to take a step back, which helps us build and nourish our character. It also can be an effective and positive outlook for us individually long term.

Chapter 9 | Success Is a Byproduct

People who work hard and focus, stay consistent and prioritize their goals will be successful. While this is what most people think, this is only the tip of the iceberg. Success is a byproduct. As a result, it is often compared to struggle. However, that is a misconception. Success is the byproduct of struggle. It is important to recognize and understand success. Perhaps, when you understand why you fell off your bike first before riding it for longer than a minute then you can understand success. Often I come across people who are striving to be successful but forget to plan, or even organize their steps to get there. Many people have the mindset to be successful but want to avoid the struggle. I've sat down with people at local coffee shops discussing how one can become successful while each remains on their own path to reach success. Interesting enough, people have told me their success stories and while each person shared a different way they got there, it all starts and ends the same way. There is no fancy or complicated way of being successful, you just have to be willing to welcome it. While success is definitely a significant part of life, and achievement, it is also up to us to learn and grow to it or within it. This process is commonly referred to as struggle. While most want to be successful, there are some who neglect the struggle, and never experience success.

As I mentioned before, many people have this idea that success and struggle are like the two sides of a coin. Either you succeed or fail in life, which again is a misconception that most people have been taught. I want to give you an alternative perspective. Crazy to think that in order to be successful, you first have to struggle. People compare their success with their peers' success, and truthfully success isn't measured the same from person to person. Be reminded everyone is responsible for how they manage their time and goals, which is why it is so important to focus on what it is you are doing, and not so much what others are doing. It can most definitely help us grow, develop, and prosper in life.

I have learned over the years that each of us has the same amount of time to accomplish just about anything we want. Unfortunately, so many people ignore key points to unlock success in life. Some of you may have listened to Adler and me on our podcast, *The best you nation*, where we are focused and dedicated to helping people, and ultimately coaching people to become more in sync with who they are on a mind/body/spirit level. In an earlier season, we focused on success and how important it is to be consistent, as well as understanding that struggling is part of the equation.

It stuck out to me when we collaborated about the idea that success is the byproduct of failure or struggle, which simply means in order for someone to be successful, one must learn to fail first so that they become consistent enough to master the obstacles of life. Most of us have goals, dreams, and ideas that we want to produce. I haven't really figured everything out, but for the most part up to this point of my life I can say I am happy with where I am at. It never stops, we are always moving forward, and the opportunity to learn will be present until we die. My dad used to say, "Fail to plan, plan to fail." Some of you may have asked how we measure success. Maybe you have asked yourself why you haven't progressed or are holding yourself back. I'll be honest it can be a bit discouraging when we don't see the change or results we want, especially if they are affecting our life. Well, here is something to think about: while it does seem a bit overwhelming to wait and be patient, be reminded that great things in life take time. You can't have a Amazon Prime membership for everything. It is nice to get those packages delivered, but sometime being patient and trusting the process will make you appreciate the moment much more.

In an earlier chapter, if you recall, I share my insight on mountains and valleys and how this analogy is so crucial to the application of life. I wanted to share an additional thought that I believe corresponds to success. I want you to imagine that you are going on a trip through the Smoky Mountains. This is your first time going and you have done all your homework to prepare for this trip. You've looked at the weather forecast, packed proper gear, acquired a map, and you are all set to go. Day one consists of about five miles of hiking until you've reached your campsite, where you set up camp for the night. It's getting a bit dark, and I am sure you are hungry. You cook yourself a hot mountain man meal to regain the calories and energy lost. You begin to prepare for the evening fire, sing a few songs with friends and wind up getting ready for bed, knowing tomorrow is going to be a brutal but beautiful day. Snuggled up and warm, you lay there listening to Mother Nature sing you a tune to fall asleep. After a while though you notice the soft patting of rain on your tent. Rain was not the projected, snow was. At this point, you probably could create the image of a camping trip in the mountains, friends gathered around the fire, and then getting into your cozy sleeping bag. Well, this was a trip I actually took last year with a buddy of mine. We had planned for this trip well in advance, making sure we had all the right gear, packed enough warm clothes and other items to make sure we would be safe while we were off the grid. Before I continue, I just wanted to point out that the five-mile hike to our first camp site was absolutely amazing. The weather was beautiful and the views were breathtaking. When we got to the camp site we set up and prepared for a cooler evening because the forecast projected snow after midnight. It didn't snow at all. What I would like to do is bring us back to the parallel between our trip and life. Every person has the "five-mile hikes" that are endlessly beautiful. We prepared ourselves and equipped for the possible detours we would face. We prepare for the circumstances, or life events as best as possible but I don't think anyone can ever really be ready with the possibility of something not going right. Even though we were prepared and well equipped, rain still managed to make its way into the tent. Success is the same way. You will prepare, plan, project what you will do at times, but you must be ready to react. I want to emphasize that even with the rain making it into the tent, it didn't change the outcome of our trip. Sometimes we allow our circumstances to affect the outcome. I call that giving up. Failing isn't giving up. Too often we see our failures as a sign of giving up. I beg to differ. Failing is the foundational piece to growth, we can fail time and time again, but consistent failure will soon become success. Giving up is the idea that I'll never reach my goal, so I'll just neglect it as a whole. Further to my point, that next morning my buddy Jon and I got up, made a quick breakfast, and decided on the game plan for the day. We knew the second day would be the coldest and most brutal part of the hike. We were facing a significant change in elevation and climate. Most of what we had was damp or wet and being on top of a mountain at fourteen degrees, there was a good chance we could have faced frostbite or hyperthermia. We decided that we would finish out the entire hike and go to Gatlinburg in the evening. Now I know this story may seem a bit irrelevant to success, but don't worry. It will make sense. Along the trail we faced major obstacles such as crossing whitewater rafting creeks that had minimal options to climb or cross over. If I remember correctly, there were thirteen total instances going up the mountain and thirteen instances coming down where we had to figure out how to get from one side of the creek to the other without falling in. Very difficult, I must admit. Despite having to get across these dangerous creeks, there was about 2,700 feet of elevation gain and incline of 14 percent most of the way. I wasn't sure how we managed to do it, but we did. This hike in the Smoky Mountains tested out manhood, our resilience, and our ability to not give in to the struggle but, rather, leverage from them. Truthfully, some of us want easy or to get from one place in life to another without working or struggling. Unfortunately, it doesn't work that way. If it were easy, I am sure everyone could do it. As much as I was ready to get back to the car and rest in a warm, cozy bed, we were only halfway done: the top of Mount Sterling, sitting at around 6,800 feet. We reached the top and what a victorious feeling to stand at the top knowing how far we came and how much we climbed. We don't realize it, but success has a tendency to start off like our hike. We face moments where we are challenged, not to crush you, however to build you. Having to find a way to accomplish something is a crafted skill and once you master it, life becomes much easier.

I also wanted to point out the valley we were in. Our campsite on day one was absolutely amazing. We didn't realize it was going to rain all night, but some would have said how horrible that was. People don't like being in the "valley" of their life. I remind and encourage people that the valley isn't a bad place in life; it's the moments in between one point and another. The dictionary definition of valley is: a low area of land between hills or mountains, typically with a river or stream flowing through it. Success isn't just the top of the mountain. Success is the whole hike. Had we not been rained on in the valley, we wouldn't have finished our hike and enjoyed time in Gatlinburg, we wouldn't have climbed up and over the mountain the way we did. My point is that each of us climbs up and over the obstacles we face in life. Some days may seem more gloomy with rain, some days it may be sunny and bright.

You can't let those moments that challenge you completely ruin or deviate your mindset.

I don't want to go too far off trail, but if you need a reminder or a recap of mountains and valleys and how you can apply the life lesson to your life, turn to chapter 3 and reread it! However, I want to be a little bit more critical about the fact that each of us is developing the algorithm for our own success. I personally believe that if you are engaging with your dreams, then you engage with your goals, and the aspirations that you are planning to see in your life.

Why do we plant seeds? So that we can grow and we can harvest and we can continue to do this cycle over and over and over and over again.

A lot of people sit and wonder why they haven't moved in their life. Progress comes from performance, which simply means if you are doing something, then something can produce. We learn to walk before we learn to run.

One thing most of us do is become too comfortable with where we are, then forget to continue and then become stagnant because when something is going good for you, then why would we want to move forward? If you are making your dream salary, or living in your dream home, that's success right? No. Success is not a finish line. Success is the big finish for the next beginning. Something we highlight on the podcast is developing a mindset to reach success by becoming aware of struggle or failure. Often we compare ourselves to one another. Look in the mirror and ask, "What am I doing to be a step closer? How can I reach my goals today?" When we stimulate our motivations, break boundaries and records, and seek to maximize our opportunities, we begin to see the progress at work. We seek results sooner than we should, which leads to discouraged and defeated people. I've mentioned this before, success is not measured the same from one person to the next. Stride at your own pace, and take it one day at a time.

When you think of potential energy, what comes to mind? I am sure the common science example of a ball at the top of the slide right? Perhaps I can shift your approach to success with the example of the ball at the top of the slide. We each have a maximum point at which we can reach our destination, however some people see their level of potential different from the next. While you may believe the top of the slide is the maximum point, some may see the middle of the slide as the maximum point. Potential is another one of those words I like to talk about. We are in control of our potential. You only know what your potential is by performing.

I would like to point out that having an expectation is also key to being successful. Being realistic with yourself, and setting a standard of accountability, will help you reach these goals or expectations. Instead of wanting to drop twenty five pounds in six months, create reachable and realistic goals like five pounds a month. People become overwhelmed when they face their Goliath of a goal. Instead, break down your major goal into a few smaller goals, and eventually you will produce the product you are looking for: success.

Something we stress a lot on the podcast is that being the best you is not a race. It is definitely not about you or your neighbor trying to get to a finish line, because your finish line is not your neighbor's finish line. Too many times I have seen people try to reach the same goal and it doesn't always work out. People have different intentions and goals, and the level of potential and interest may vary for each person. For example, being a millionaire isn't everyone's expectation in life. Somebody who's content with making $90,000 a year may just be perfectly fine. Some of us want to have millions of dollars or drive a nice car. It all sounds nice, but not everyone sees that in their success plan. It's about being content. There are no limitations to how content someone is. You have to choose to live your life to the best that you can for you and not for anyone else. That's why we who inspire people, we inspire people based off personal experiences. Yes, I read books. Yes, I read articles. Yes, I listen to podcasts. But that doesn't mean that that's determining my life. I get to choose if I'm going to listen, I get to choose whether I'm going to want to change. These things happen because we as people have to develop a mindset for ourselves. Be a little selfish sometimes with your growth, because too many times, we find ourselves wanting to grow for the people around us that we love, the people that we spend time with, the people that we work with. And then when we really sit back and we realize, oh my gosh, who did I really do this for? We end up dissatisfied or disappointed. Let me put it into perspective. Instead of working a job to only be promoted, work your job because you are passionate or motivated to make a difference. It's more fulfilling to know you didn't do it for others, but you did it for you.

Mediocrity is common, and it's up to us if we want more. Being the best at being you is an achievable goal, because you are focused on bettering you. Why do so many people feel like they have to have a restart? Life is too short to restart to become successful. Instead of asking where do I begin, ask yourself where do I continue. You've been working on you every day since you've been born. That day was your beginning. Sometimes we hit pause, and we need to hit play again to keep on going. The content posture isn't going to change you. It's the get up, go out and make it happen mindset that gets us to the next level of life.

Being comfortable doesn't give us the opportunity to learn more about ourselves. While I am not discounting comfort, I am only pointing out that we shouldn't stop moving forward because we reached our goals, we should stay proactive and set new goals to keep striving.

I've always brought up the saying "Life is a marathon." You are not racing against other people. You're racing against yourself. Ten thousand people show up to an event to run twenty-six miles and get a fancy medal for completing, not winning. Winning is when it's all said and done, when your story comes to an end, and your time has come. Success is the byproduct of struggle. We live and we learn. Learning that failing or struggling is part of the process, becoming familiar with what it is like to be uncomfortable sometimes, it brings you to a better understanding of what life is about. We learn to ride a bike not because we jump on and go; we learn to ride a bike because we fell multiple times before we mastered riding a bike. Consistency is key when it comes to becoming successful.

Chapter 10 | Final Steps

You know, I remember when I first started writing this book, I had absolutely no idea where I would begin. I have never wrapped my mind around the idea of writing a book.

Over the years of writing, I have learned a lot about myself. Being able to communicate with people, and vocalize the moments of my life that were difficult while still being able to relate with people, this is what I live for. It has never been about just writing a story, it was making a personal connection with my readers. I have no background in journalism, or novel writing. I wanted to change the standards for writing. I wanted to make sure this was like a dialogue. My part is here in this book, while you read you are creating those touch points and connections.

As of right now, everything that I have experienced from the time I was born to right now, it's given me the opportunity to share a story, share the moments that got me to where I am today, and being vulnerable with you makes this writing experience that much more meaningful to me.

I think that success and vulnerability are vital aspects of our individual growth and well-being. Being successful is nothing more than having an understanding of struggle. As I mentioned before, you don't learn to ride a bike by just riding the bike. You learn to ride a bike because you fell off over and over again. Eventually you found a way to balance, ride, and keep going on that bike. It then becomes second nature for us.

You know, someone once asked me, why are you writing this book? Why are you even approaching this kind of conversation with somebody? And I said, well, honestly speaking, this book can impact anybody. You don't have to be adopted to read this book. You don't have to be somebody who's been in an orphanage or has experienced trauma to understand these concepts. This book is intended for everybody because every single one of us has experienced life.

Every single one of us has gone through something that has pulled us down and has made us think, has made us respond a certain way. So anybody who's been through something can find some relevant content within this book. In these chapters that I've written here, these are bits and pieces of my life that I want to share because I felt like this is important. There is no self-gain here, simply impact. This is me sharing with you that you can go through something. You can be at the wrong part of your life. And no matter how raw it is, you're still amazing. It's easier said than done because everybody wants to hear what you're doing, but it's how I got here. I'm in my twenty's. I'm an

EMT. I work at one of the largest hospital organizations across the nation. Never did I think I'd end up where I am, but through the process of breakthrough, and beating those odds, I was able to have clarity of my purpose.

I'm hoping God will bring clarity through this book. I believe that we all have a purpose here on earth. Through the works we do, we can reach people. I didn't think a book would be the way, but when I started, I knew this would be the way God was going to use my story. I am praying that this book brings light into your life. This book is going to hit everybody personally and differently.
All of us are going to approach our circumstances differently because each of us has a different perception. And that's what makes this book so unique. I get to share my experience with you. I get to share with you the lessons that I had to learn and put them in a book where you get to kind of pick pieces out of me, like the story that I share with you, with the guy at the coffee shop and sitting down and recognizing that.

We all have the same opportunity to push past this and have these vulnerable moments where we can learn and say, well, I've been here, I need to forgive myself and move forward. That's the part that I am emphasizing so much throughout this book. It's finding the place in your heart to forgive yourself, and begin to heal.

I believe this book is going to reach millions of people, because it has bits and pieces that are going to impact you in life. It's going to impact people around you. It's going to give you a way to relate. I've had to learn to execute and I've had to learn to just dig deeper into my own story and understand that everything that I've gone through is my story.

People are going to think that I'm crazy. And it's like, well, you haven't been in my shoes. While that mindset should be everyone's. This is why we don't share or speak about our stories. Because not each person will understand exactly what you have been thorough. However, we all have been through an experience that created a path for us. We may not wear the same shoes, but both pairs of shoes serve the same purpose. You don't know what it's like to have to defend yourself or fend for yourself as an infant. But you know me as me. Each of you shares unique relationship, experiences, memories and that's important to me.

You are amazing and you have the same opportunity to be the best version of yourself as anybody else in this world. There's 7 billion of us. We're all unique. We all have our own idea of life. And sometimes it's great to tap into other people's seasoning. Our own food is amazing. And sometimes when we try somebody else's food, they use a different seasoning that we're not used to. Somebody else may not cook chicken the same way as me, but sometimes it's nice to try chicken a different way or different seasoning on the chicken, and in parallel to life, sometimes it's nice to hear what others have to say about life.

The experiences that you've had are no worse or better than other people's experiences. They're unique. Your experiences don't overpopulate or become annoying or whatever the case may be. They're just unique. You've got to find that balance. You get to find that within yourself and say, "Oh, it's OK. It's OK." That's what's so exclusive about being vulnerable, that's what's so exclusive about being ourselves and having the opportunity to share and be ourselves.

I have given myself three years to put something together, and this past year I really had to find time to dig deeper and deeper and deeper into parts of my life that I didn't necessarily want to share. And it's made me better because of it, it's given me perception and perspective about other people in their life, it's made me understand that everybody has something that they're struggling with. And a lot of times we hide them and we run away from them.

And hiding from our struggles does not really promote healing. It simply promotes a temporary halt on growth, on healing, even on forgiveness. Therefore, I encourage you as you're finding out who you are and you look yourself in the mirror, remind yourself that your story matters. Your journey is a beautiful one. While everyone is on their own path, we all have experiences that connect us to a degree.

Why don't we take down those boxes of brokenness that have been sitting on our shelves for five, ten, fifteen years and begin to forgive ourselves and find that moment of vulnerability with yourself, recognizing the power of healing, feeling the weight fall off your shoulders. You will start to recognize that you've struggled with, but you can overcome it. You can get past this. You have already gotten past it.

There are probably things in that box that you wrote down that you were struggling with and you didn't even know it, but you overcame and you bypassed because that's just who we are. We have those moments where we trigger the events and the events trigger us and we somehow get past them. And then you realize, "Wow, I did overcome. I already got past this." And it motivates you to continue to strive for the best version of who you are, because that is what we live for.

That's what gives us this opportunity. So, I hope that each of you, as you read this book, as you close out this book, walk away with this: You get to be you. And you have to embrace that your story is not my story and my story is not your story. You will hear victory. You will hear what it sounds like to be healing. What it sounds like to be confident, to restore finances, to restore a relationship, restore friendships, restore brotherhood, restore education, to restore emotional imbalance, to restore whatever the case may be.

Don't hide from what you've been hurt by. Learn to embrace, let go, forgive. And use your story to impact people. Believe me, more people want to hear what you have to say because they want to relate to somebody and learn from somebody.

Author's Note

My name is Finn Foster and it is a humbling experience to have been able to write this book. I remember the first time I started brainstorming my ideas, feels so long ago. I started writing this book about four years ago after coming home from the Airforce. Through the years I had the opportunity to learn more about myself and learn about people along the way. I used to think writing a book would be beyond my reach, but I conquered the impossible. Each of us has a story to share, and I hope as you venture through life, you will continue to focus on becoming the best version of yourself. I know it can be discouraging at times, maybe even scary. Don't give up. Learn everything you can about anything, and be willing to make strides in the forward direction. You and I both have the same 24 hours to make our dreams come true. My journey is definitely one I can look back on and embrace. growing up wasn't easy, but I made it. Learning to change and be okay with being uncomfortable were crucial lessons in life, As you look back, be reminded it's only to see how far you have come. Don't look back for to long, focus on what's ahead and start setting your goals for how you'll reach them. I hope this book shared its purpose to testify the life of a troubled child who learned to love and to live a Christ like life. Remember it's not perfection its progress when it comes to life. Become the person you want to become each day by learning to embrace all of you, to live life with a purpose, and come to a peace of mind about vulnerability. Forgive yourself and begin to watch your life prosper more than ever. Until the next book, I hope this book impacted you in some way! May you be blessed.

Finn Foster

* 9 7 8 0 5 7 8 9 1 6 4 3 9 *